BOUNCE BACK

God is our refuge and strength, an ever-present help in trouble. Psalm 46:1

WHATEVER HAPPENS, YOU TOO CAN

BOUNCE BACK

39 HEART-LIFTING, HOPE-BUILDING
STORIES OF SOME WHO DID

— COMPILED BY —
DIANA L. JAMES

HORIZON BOOKS
CAMP HILL, PENNSYLVANIA

Horizon Books
3825 Hartzdale Drive, Camp Hill, PA 17011

ISBN: 0-88965-139-6
LOC: 97-70111
© 1997 by Diana L. James
Printed in the United States of America

97 98 99 00 01   5 4 3 2

Unless otherwise indicated Scripture
references taken from the HOLY BIBLE:
NEW INTERNATIONAL VERSION.®
©1973, 1978, 1984
by the International Bible Society.
Used by permission of
Zondervan Publishing House.
All rights reserved.

Scripture references labeled "KJV" are from the
HOLY BIBLE: KING JAMES VERSION.

Scripture references labeled "TLB" are from
THE LIVING BIBLE. © 1971,
by Tyndale House Publishers.

Scripture references labeled "RSV" are from the
REVISED STANDARD VERSION of the Bible,
© 1946, 1952, 1971 and 1973
by the Division of Christian Education
of the National Council of the Churches of Christ
in the United States of America.

To my irrepressible brother
David O. Carter
and my beloved mother,
Lillian Carter Jacobs,
who taught me by her example
that if you walk with God
you can bounce back.

Contents

10 Bounce Back More than Once

11 Bounce Back from Harbored Resentment

12 Help Others Bounce Back

Acknowledgments

I want to thank my husband, Max James, for his editing assistance and loving support.

And thanks to all of you who so generously contributed stories to be used in *Bounce Back* because you believe in the message of this book.

INTRODUCTION

This book presents a collection of stories told by people from various walks of life. In these pages, you will meet real people, sharing real experiences. Many are published writers; several are well-known speakers; some are pastors or ministers; others have little or no writing or speaking experience—but *all* have a story to tell.

Some of the accounts related here involve life-changing occurences. Others deal with events that may seem trivial at first glance, but, upon further reflection, carry deeper messages. Some are humorous, others poignant. From the lofty to the mundane, these narrations reveal insights gained by people who have suffered setbacks, faced perplexity or perhaps made mistakes, but with God's help, have found renewal and peace.

Each story illustrates a facet of the many ways in which God gives His healing, His forgiveness, His comfort and His love.

This book has two main purposes: The first is to give hope and encouragement to those who are presently caught in a seemingly hopeless situation in life. The second is to help the reader build a solid foundation of faith in God's promises and His grace.

In sunshine or storm, my prayer is that your heart will be lifted as you read these true stories and that you will know in your spirit that whatever befalls you, with God's help, you too can bounce back!

CHAPTER 1

BOUNCE BACK FROM FEAR

The way to overcome fear is to get close to God. As we seek the Lord, thanking Him daily for His goodness, our trust in Him grows stronger. When we sincerely surrender our fears to Him, placing everything in His loving care, He fills our hearts with peace. The stories in this chapter illustrate how the writers, each in a different way, used that approach to conquer their fears and to renew their lives.

> *The LORD is my light and my salvation—whom shall I fear? The LORD is the stronghold of my life—of whom shall I be afraid?*
>
> *(Psalm 27:1)*

Handing the Gavel to God

Florence Littauer

"Will I ever be able to speak in public again?" I asked myself as I stared at my reflection in the mirror. After five weeks in the hospital with the strain of operations, medical blunders and much too much medication, my body was limp, my face haggard, my mind fuzzy.

Worst of all, I was consumed by the fear that my concentration, my memory, my strength and my healthy appearance would never return.

Earlier that year, at age thirty-five, I had committed my life to Jesus Christ. But I had only taken a few baby steps in my Christian walk when I was sidelined by my long and harrowing hospital experience. Grasping for anything to relieve my fears about the future, I reached for my Bible and opened it to Second Timothy 1:7—"For God

hath not given us the spirit of fear; but of power,
and of love, and of a sound mind" (KJV).

As I pondered that verse, I began to analyze my
fears. I was stunned to realize that they were all
about myself—not about Fred or the children, not
about business or home or war or famine. My
fears seemed to focus on my personal future and
my desire to achieve, excel and conquer new
worlds.

A disturbing thought flashed through my mind:
What difference does it make? Were Fred and the
children breathlessly awaiting my return to the
Women's League, the Little Theatre and the Club
circuit? Had these organizations fallen apart and
been forced to close down in my absence? With
honesty and a dose of disquieting humility, I had
to answer, *No.* Then did it really matter if I never
got going at top speed again?

I asked myself, *Would my family love me the same
if I never returned to being a human dynamo?* The
humbling answer was, *Yes.—In fact, they might even
love me more!*

I reread the same Scripture verse later that day,
and a disturbing realization began to form in my
mind. It wasn't my family who had given up on
me; it wasn't God; it was the person I always see
in the mirror. I was the one who could not accept
me as a plain person stripped of titles and high positions.

I had always equated success and busyness with
happiness. Now it seemed the Lord was showing
me that my days of succeeding through my own

strength and leadership were finished. I'd better hand over my gavel and trust my future to Him. I wasn't really willing, but it seemed I had no choice.

I continued to study the Bible, seeking to apply the words of Scripture directly to my own life, as I had been learning to do as a new and eager Christian. One day, I strained and struggled over a familiar passage, First Corinthians 13:5.

I read that "love does not keep a record of wrongs." I understood it, but I wondered how it applied to me. As I asked that question, the answer came: *You have kept a record in your mind of everything Fred has ever done wrong.*

I tried to proclaim my innocence, but God showed me that I had kept this record of Fred's wrongs in my mind for the thirteen years we had been married and that I had mentally reviewed it every day while I washed the dishes.

From the time I was a child, I had an innate talent for straightening out other people. I could spot their faults and show them how to improve if only they would listen to me. Fred, on the other hand, had been told from birth that he was God's perfect child. Is it any wonder that we both entered the marriage expecting the other to be grateful for winning such a prize?

This unreality had resulted in a constant battle of wills, each of us believing that everything should go our own way. I had submitted on the surface, but underneath I had become more resentful and rebellious over the years. Reviewing the growing record of Fred's wrongs each night as I did the dishes gave me a sort of fiendish pleasure and a perverse kind of comfort for the slights I felt.

It seemed an innocent enough way to entertain myself while doing a chore I didn't enjoy. But now here was God pointing out to me through His Word that, as a dutiful wife, I was to love my husband and that I couldn't love him at the same time I was keeping a record of his wrongs—not even the ones that seemed unforgivable.

It dawned on me that being a real Christian was going to be a lot harder than I had expected. In spite of that, I began right away to pray that God would remove the list of Fred's wrongs from my mind and that I would be able to do the dishes without reviewing it any more. A thirteen-year-old habit is hard to break, but gradually the list began to disappear—at least until Fred made me angry. Then it would start all over again.

It occurred to me one evening, as I stood with my hands in the dishwater, that I could start a list of Fred's "rights" to think about instead of thinking about his wrongs. I copied Philippians 4:8 and tacked it on a cabinet door where I could see it while washing dishes: "Whatsoever things are *true*, whatsoever things are *honest*, whatsoever things are *just*, *whatsoever things are pure*, whatsoever things are lovely, whatsoever things are of *good report*; if there be any *virtue*, and if there be any *praise*, think on these things" (KJV, emphasis mine).

I began to think on Fred's positives instead of his negatives. I knew he was honest, just and pure; he had many virtuous qualities that were worthy of praise. But I didn't feel much like praising him because he rarely praised me. After all, shouldn't *he* be the one to go first?

The more I studied the Scriptures, the more flexible and relaxed I became. I stopped looking for Fred-related projects and goals. As I became willing to replace my list of Fred's wrongs with a list of his good qualities, I became more willing to sit back and let the Lord Jesus lead—not only in matters relating to my marriage but also on projects and goals in general. Only *then* did He begin to remove the spirit of fear and to restore my strength, my mind—and my love.

Looking back, I see that God allowed me to become weak so that I would learn to depend on His strength. Have there been times in your life when you were discouraged, depressed or fearful and felt you could never bounce back? I know how you feel, because I've been there too.

During my "time out" on the sidelines, when I was in the pit of dejection, fear and resentment, a transition took place. I learned to depend not on myself but on God. He showed me that He could handle my life just as well as I could—maybe even better. In retrospect, I realize that God would have kept me weak and fearful for a much longer time if I hadn't learned to give Him control of my life so that He could teach me how to bounce back—according to His plan.

FLORENCE LITTAUER is president and founder of CLASS (Christian Leaders, Authors and Speakers Seminar), Inc. She is a best-selling author of twenty-four books. With her husband Fred, she travels nationally and internationally as a Christian speaker, sharing her trademark humor and valuable insights. Florence is also in demand as a radio and TV talk show guest and keynote speaker for retreats, business conventions and seminars. Between their travels, Florence and Fred reside in Palm Springs, California.

What Would They Do without Me?

Lola D. Gillebaard

If your kids are anything like mine, they believe their parents will always be around. They can't even stand for you to get sick. You're supposed to be there always, no matter what. Big babies, that's what they are!

Like many moms, I've always worried and feared for my kids. You know how it is: They may be six feet tall and approaching their thirties, as mine are, but they're still our "little" boys. If anything came along that threatened to hurt any of them in any way, I panicked. Like any good momma bear, my instinct was: "I've got to protect my cubs!"

Once in a while though, something happens that changes everything and gives you a whole new perspective. Like what happened when I found out I had breast cancer.

When I broke the news to my husband Hank,

my composure flew out the window and I burst
out crying. This was pretty hard on Hank, and I
didn't want to do that again with my four sons. I
fretted and wondered how I could tell them in a
way that would not cause them trauma and dis-
tress. After due consideration, I decided to follow
our usual family custom and just *blurt it out!*

Here's what happened when the first son called
on the phone:

"Hi, Mom."

"Hi, babe."

"How are you?"

"Not too good. The doctor says I've got cancer." Long silence.

"Gosh, does that mean you're going to die?"

Then the second son called.

"Hi, Mom."

"Hi, babe."

"What's up?"

"Nothing good, I'm afraid. I just found out I
have breast cancer." Long silence.

"But, Mom, why? You don't eat fat."

By the time the third son called, I was getting
the routine down pat:

"Hi, Mom."

"Hi, babe."

"What's new?"

"Nothing good. I've just been told I have cancer." Long silence.

"I hope this doesn't upset Dad."

I could hardly wait to hear what the fourth son
would say. Finally he called:

"Hi, Mom."

"Hi, babe."

"How's life treating you?"

"Not so hot. The doctor says I have breast cancer." Long silence.

"Darn. Why couldn't it have been Mrs. Walcott?" (Mrs. Walcott lived down the street from us and used to chase all the kids off her sidewalk yelling and brandishing her broom.)

Those deflating phone conversations took place on December 4, 1987, just before the Christmas season was getting into full swing. The next day, Saturday, I was to go in for a chest X-ray and bone scan as a preliminary to a mastectomy scheduled for Monday. I told my family that if the doctors found the cancer had spread through my body, I would refuse the surgery.

Hank said he would stay with me during the X-ray and bone scan. Now if anyone knows Hank, I know Hank. It worries me how he worries. I didn't want him out there in the waiting room pacing up and down, wearing holes in the hospital carpeting. I told him I could handle it just fine, thank you.

Saturday came and I kept my lab appointment—without Hank. All day long, it seemed I did nothing but take off my clothes and put them on again. Off—on. Off—on. "So this is what it's like to be a model," I mumbled to myself.

I underwent each test inside a cubicle that would have made an igloo seem cozy and warm. The nurses glided in and out on their squeakless shoes, taking X-rays or poking needles in my arms. Then they were gone, leaving me alone in my igloo, shivering with cold and terror.

My goose bumps were getting goose bumps when finally a group of long-faced men in white coats arrived to peer at me and prod me with their icy hands. After they left, I sat in numb fear, waiting for the doctor to come back and tell me the verdict. Had the cancer spread? The chances, I had been told, were 50-50 that it had.

Oddly, I began to realize that my fears were not about me. As usual, they were for my sons. I wondered what they would do if something happened to me. I thought of times they had disagreed and argued with each other and with their dad. I wondered how they would get along if I died and there was no longer a full-time peacemaker in the family.

I tried to pray. The prayer had trouble getting past the knot of terror in my throat. I began to picture my funeral. I saw our church with my family all sitting in the front row. There were flowers everywhere. Someone was reading the Twenty-third Psalm: "The LORD is my shepherd; I shall not want. . . ." The words that got to me were: "Yea, though I walk through the valley of the shadow of death, I will fear no evil: for thou art with me" (KJV). Those words stood out. They spoke to my soul. I repeated them quietly to myself, over and over. The room began to feel warmer, and the knot in my throat began to melt away.

Then suddenly the doctor was there. His voice, like the voice of an angel, flowed over me like a healing balm. "I see no sign of cancer in the rest of your body," he said.

I prayed that his vision was 20/20!

My spirits soared as I drove home. I wheeled into the driveway, jumped out of the car and ran toward our front door. The sound of music wafted from our living room. Mahalia Jackson was there singing "Silent Night." (Well, it *sounded* like she was there.) I dashed inside. Standing in the corner of the living room was the largest Christmas tree we'd ever had. It was decorated with every orna-ment the kids had ever made—even the ugly ones.

Imagine, all this three weeks before Christmas, and I'd been away at the hospital lab for only five hours!

There, lined up in front of that huge tree, was my family. To my amazement, each one was wearing a suit and tie! I pushed back the thought that they looked ready to carry me down the aisle of the church—laid out in a box.

"Merry Christmas, Mom," they shouted in uni-son.

"Merry Christmas," I smiled, "and Happy New Year. We've got many more to come."

Hank and the boys and I all hugged each other as we sniffled and wiped away our tears. My four sons seemed suddenly taller, wiser and more ma-ture.

In the midst of all this commotion, a great peace came over me. I wasn't fearful for my boys any more. A prayer silently formed inside me: *Thank You, dear God, thank You! I got Your message. You're always with me—and with my family. You've always been here, even when we "walked through the valley of the shadow of death."*

Then I noticed the dining room table was set with our best china, the good silver and all our precious chipped crystal.

I can tell it was one of the best evenings we've ever had together. God had never seemed so near. The family had never seemed so capable and caring. And take-out pizza had never tasted so good!

 LOLA D. GILLEBAARD is, first and foremost, a humorist. She believes that laughter is the handshake of good communication and that humor in business is serious business. She is college professor, author and professional speaker. As a writer Lola has received the *Reader's Digest* Writer's Award. As a speaker she conducts training seminars on humor in the workplace and frequently serves as keynote speaker for corporate and convention audiences. She is a past president of the Greater Los Angeles Chapter of the National Speakers Association.

Pressure + Prayer = Peace

Pam Stephens

It was a Friday afternoon in February and, even for Southern California, there was a definite chill in the air. My friend and I had just walked into my kitchen from outside. I put a teakettle on the stove to boil so that we could have a warm cup of tea. We sat down to talk about our lives: the kids, our husbands and the neighborhood events coming up. We were both looking forward to watching the Winter Olympics on TV that weekend. Our conversation was interrupted by my five-year-old daughter, Jenny.

Jenny had strep throat and I was treating her according to the doctor's instructions. We felt she was responding well. But now she was showing me a blister several inches long on her neck. Immediately I called the doctor but was informed he had left early that day and wouldn't be available all weekend. His assistant would be taking his calls. The assistant phoned me and assured me Jenny would be fine until Monday, when they could see her in the office.

By Saturday morning more blisters were forming. She had one under each arm and on several other warm spots. There was also a red ring completely around her neck. Once again I phoned the doctor's exchange and received the same response.

In hindsight, I know I should have insisted the doctor see her, but I wasn't wise enough to know I could take charge of my own child's health, and I was too young to realize that doctors aren't infallible!

On Monday morning we met the doctor at the door to his office. The older, more experienced doctor immediately knew the condition was serious. He told us she must be hospitalized right away. Then he picked up our precious blond Jenny and carried her across the street to the hospital.

My husband and I followed, fearful and confused about how this had happened. They admitted Jenny and we watched, gripped with fear, as they donned hospital gowns and masks and placed her in reverse isolation. We too were draped so that we would not contaminate the now-opened blisters which left raw, exposed skin.

They soaked her four times a day in saline solution. Salt. Open wounds. They treated her much as they do a burn victim. Finally a name was given to this madness: Stevens-Johnson Syndrome, an allergic reaction to strep or to the medications treating it. It was a rarity in the medical field, and many residents and nurses came into Jenny's room those first few days to see it firsthand.

This of course was even more frightening for Jenny and for us. The soaking was extremely painful to Jenny. "Mommy," she cried out, "please don't let them do that to me again!" There was nothing I could do to keep it from hurting. I felt helpless and out of control.

We tried to make her as comfortable as possible. We smothered her with love and attention and stayed with her all day and long into the night. We were in Jenny's hospital room two full days before I finally walked out into the hall to take a break. I paced up and down the corridor, back and forth, trying to understand, trying to get a grip on my emotions.

I had been memorizing Scripture verses such as, "Do not be anxious about anything, but in everything, by prayer and petition, with thanksgiving, present your requests to God. And the peace of God, which transcends all understanding, will guard your hearts and your minds in Christ Jesus" (Philippians 4:6-7). I cried out to God, *"Don't be anxious about anything?" This isn't fair! I don't understand this! Why her? She's suffering, and I can't stand to see her suffer!*

Like that teakettle I had put on the stove to make tea for my friend and me, the flame was up high, and pretty soon the water began to bubble and boil. I had worked up a pretty good head of steam.

But then I changed the tone of my prayer. I said, *Please heal her, Lord. I want to take her home with me, but if You choose to take her home to be with You, then I give You my permission. I know You love her even more than I do, so I will trust You.* I must tell you that God didn't need my permission for anything. He is God! But I felt such a relief after releasing Jenny to Him.

Something miraculous happened after I prayed that prayer. It was as though I had removed the lid from the teakettle and let all the built-up steam come out—whoosh! My prayer to God relieved the anxiety that filled my heart with fear.

Jenny was in the hospital for one whole week. We could have lost her if the blisters had attacked her lungs, causing more disastrous complications. But God chose not to allow that.

She went back to kindergarten five weeks later. God was good, but God would have been a good God even if He had chosen to take Jenny to live with Him in heaven. She was healed completely and has no scars, which we feel was a real miracle and blessing. Jenny is a grown woman now. She points back to that time as the moment when she knew God was real and that He had a plan for her life.

Are you feeling fearful and pressured by a situation or a crisis in your life? Are you getting "steamed up"? Maybe you need to take the lid off and release it to God through prayer. Relinquish it to God's control. He's in control anyway. Do you need peace today? Do you feel as though someone were rubbing "saline" into your deep wounds? The healing process often causes pain, but often it is the only way to bring restoration and complete healing to the affliction.

During this time with my daughter's illness, I learned firsthand that God was not only in control of my life, but also the lives of my children. I learned to focus on the *who* of life, not the *what* of life. I learned that prayer releases the pressure of fear and gives me peace. Prayer can relieve your pressure too! It is as close as the next whisper of His name—Jesus!

PAM STEPHENS is a speaker for Christian conferences and retreats, where she uses humor to teach the deep lessons of life. She has taught Bible Studies, both locally and nationally, since 1980. Pam is part of the teaching staff with Florence Littauer's CLASS (Christian Leaders, Authors and Speakers Seminars), Inc. She and her husband live in Lake Arrowhead, California. They have two grown daughters and a grandson.

CHAPTER 2

BOUNCE BACK FROM ANGER

A nger, whether in the form of a flash eruption or a long smoldering resentment, can be a debilitating force in our lives if we give rein to it. The four stories in this chapter give examples of how anger can be overcome if it is totally surrendered to God.

Man's anger does not bring about the righteous life that God desires. (James 1:20)

The Healing Power of Forgiveness

Karen O'Connor

I thought about her. I dreamed about her. I saw her in every woman I met. Some had her name, Cathy. Others had her deep-set blue eyes or her curly dark hair. Even the slightest resemblance twisted my stomach into a knot.

Weeks, months, years passed. Was I never to be free of this woman who had gone after my husband and ultimately married him? I couldn't go on like this. The endless rage, resentment, guilt and anger drained the life out of everything I did. I went to counseling. I attended self-help classes, seminars, workshops. I read books. I talked to anyone who would listen.

I ran. I walked the beach. I drove for miles to nowhere. I screamed into my pillow at night. I meditated. I prayed. I blamed myself. I did everything I knew how to do—except surrender.

Then one Saturday in 1982, I was drawn to a day-long seminar on the healing power of forgiveness sponsored by a church in my neighborhood. After some discussion and sharing, participants were asked to close their eyes, then locate someone in their lives they had not forgiven—for whatever reason, real or imagined.

Next, the leader invited us to look at whether or not we'd be willing to forgive that person. My first thought was Cathy. My stomach churned again. My hands were suddenly wet, and my head throbbed. I felt I had to get out of that room, but something kept me in my seat.

How could I forgive a person like Cathy? Not only had she hurt me, but she'd hurt my children. So I turned my attention to other people in my life. My mother. She'd be easy to forgive. Or my friend Ann or my former high school English teacher. Anyone but Cathy. But there was no escape. The name persisted, and her face grew large in my mind.

Then a voice within gently asked, *Are you ready to let go of this? To release her? To forgive yourself as well?*

I turned hot, then cold. I began to shake. I was certain everyone around me could hear my heart beating. Yes, I was willing. I couldn't hold onto my anger any longer. It was killing me. In that moment, without doing anything else, an incredible shift in my perception took place. I simply let go!

I can't describe it. I don't know what happened or what prompted me at that moment to do something I had resisted so doggedly for months. All I know is that for the first time in four years I completely surrendered to the Holy Spirit. I released my grip on Cathy, my ex-husband, myself. I let go of the anger—just like that.

Within seconds, energy rushed through every cell of my body. My mind became alert, my heart lightened. I saw things I had not seen before. Suddenly I realized that as long as I separate myself from even one person, I separate myself from God.

How "righteous" I had been! How arrogant and possessive! How important it had been for me to be right, no matter what the cost! And it had cost me plenty—my health, my spontaneity, my aliveness.

I had no idea what was next, but it didn't matter. That night I slept straight through till morning. No dreams. No haunting face. No reminders.

If it had been up to me alone, I don't know if I would have had the courage or the generosity to make the first move. But it was not up to me. There was no mistaking the power of the Holy Spirit within me.

The following Monday I walked into my office and wrote Cathy a letter. The words spilled onto the page without effort.

"Dear Cathy," I began. "On Saturday morning . . . ," and I proceeded to tell her what had occurred.

I told her how I had deliberately continued to separate myself from her, to judge her for what she had done and, as a result, how I denied both of us the healing power of forgiveness.

On Wednesday afternoon of the same week, the phone rang.

"Karen?"

There was no mistaking the voice.

"It's Cathy," she said softly.

Surprisingly my stomach remained calm. My hands were dry. My voice was steady and sure. I listened more than I talked—unusual for me. I found myself actually interested in what Cathy had to say.

She thanked me for the letter, and she acknowledged my courage in writing it. Then she told me how sorry she was—for everything. She talked briefly about her regret, her sadness for me and more. All I had ever wanted to hear from her she said that day.

As I replaced the receiver, however, I realized that as nice as it was to hear her words of apology, they didn't really matter. They paled in comparison to what God was teaching me. Buried deep in the trauma of my divorce was the truth I had been looking for all my life without even knowing it. *God is my source, my strength, my very supply.* He alone can minister healing.

For four years I had been caught in the externals, the reasons, the lies, the excuses, the jealousy, the anger. But now I had a clear experience of what had formerly been a stack of psychological insights. Now I really knew that no one can hurt me as long as I am in God's hands. No one can take my good away. No one can rob me of my life—unless I allow it.

My life is mine and every experience, no matter how painful or confusing it seems, can serve my spiritual growth. Every moment has its purpose if I am serving the Lord.

Since then I have started over again in another city—free of the binding ties of jealousy, anger and resentment, free to experience all that God has for me.

" 'For I know the plans I have for you,' declares the LORD, 'plans to prosper you and not to harm you, plans to give you hope and a future' " (Jeremiah 29:11).

KAREN O'CONNOR is an award-winning author/speaker known for her inspiring books and presentations on a variety of topics from "women and money" to "intimacy in relationships." She has appeared on national radio and television shows including *The Sally Jesse Raphael Show* and *The 700 Club*. Karen is also a writing consultant and an experienced seminar leader for schools, churches and professional organizations. She lives with her husband in San Diego, California.

I Don't Really Want to Hurt My Child

Kathy Collard Miller

Darcy's training pants were wet again. Again!

Marching over to my two-year-old daughter, I directed her into the bathroom. As I struggled to pull down the soaking pants, I felt a rush of frustration and a sense of failure.

"Darcy, you're supposed to come in the bathroom and go in the potty chair. Why can't you learn?" I continued to berate her. As I began spanking her with my hand, my tension and tiredness found an outlet. Spanking turned to hitting.

Darcy's uncontrollable screaming brought me back to reason. Seeing the red welt on her bottom, I dropped to my knees.

"How can I act this way?" I sobbed. "I love Jesus. I don't really want to hurt my child. Oh God, please help me."

The rest of that day I held my anger in check.
The next day started out pleasantly. I watched my
happy daughter. *How could I ever be angry with you
or want to hurt you?*

But as the day progressed and pressures closed
in on me, I became impatient. I looked forward to
a few moments of peace while Darcy and two-
month-old Mark took their naps.

Telling Darcy to play quietly in her room, I
rocked Mark to sleep. Just as I laid him carefully
into his crib, Darcy burst into the room shouting,
"Mommy, I want to color."

Mark woke up crying. I grabbed Darcy by the
shoulders, shook her and screamed, "Shut up!
Shut up! I want him to go to sleep!"

Both Darcy and Mark cried as I shoved Darcy
aside, rushed out of the bedroom and stomped
through the house, banging walls and slamming
doors. Only after I kicked a kitchen cupboard and
dented it did my anger subside.

As the weeks turned into months, my anger
habit worsened. At times I grew so violent that I
hit my toddler on the head. Other times I kicked
her or slapped her face.

As a Christian for ten years, I was ashamed. *Oh
God,* I prayed over and over again, *please take away
my anger.* Yet no matter how much I prayed, I
could not control my anger when Darcy didn't
perform according to my desires. I wondered
whether I would kill Darcy in one of my next
rages. In time, I had to be honest with myself.
God, I'm a child abuser! Help me!

I was afraid to tell my husband, Larry. *After all, he's a policeman. He's arresting people for the very things I'm doing.* I certainly couldn't tell my friends either. What would they think of me? I led a Bible study. I was looked up to as a strong Christian woman. But inside I was screaming for help.

One day I realized Larry had left his off-duty service revolver in the bureau drawer. Convinced God no longer loved me and had given up on me, I concluded suicide was the only answer. Then I wouldn't hurt Darcy any more. But then the thought sprang into my mind: *But if people hear that a Christian like me committed suicide, what will they think of Jesus?* I couldn't bear the thought that Jesus' name would be maligned, even if I wasn't acting much like a Christian.

Even though suicide was no longer an option, I didn't have any hope. God didn't answer my prayers for an instantaneous deliverance of my anger, so He must not care. I was in a pit of despair and depression.

One day, I shared briefly with a neighbor friend about my anger. She didn't condemn me as another friend had when I'd tried to share my pain. She even indicated she felt angry toward her children too. *Oh Lord, maybe there's hope for me after all,* I cried out when I left her house that day.

From that point on, God seemed to break through my despair and little by little revealed the underlying causes and the solutions for my anger. And there were many. I had to learn how to identify my anger before it became destructive. I forced myself to believe God wanted to forgive me—over and over again. Reading books about disciplining children effectively, I became more consistent in responding calmly to Darcy's disobedience. She became better behaved.

I also copied verses like Ephesians 4:31 and Proverbs 10:12 onto cards, placing them in various locations throughout the house. As I took Darcy into the bathroom, I would be reminded: "Hatred stirs up dissension, but love covers over all wrongs" (Proverbs 10:12). These verses helped to break my cycle of anger.

Eventually I had the courage to share my problem with my Bible study group. James 5:16 admonishes us to "confess your sins to each other and pray for each other so that you may be healed." They prayed for me and their prayers indeed had wonderful results.

Through a difficult process of growth over a year, God's Holy Spirit empowered me to be the loving, patient mother to Darcy that I wanted to be. I learned many principles during that time that I now share in the parenting books I've written, like *When Counting to Ten Isn't Enough*. I also teach parenting seminars.

I'm thankful to the Lord for healing the relationship between Darcy and me. Now a beautiful twenty-one-year-old, Darcy has forgiven me for the way I treated her. We share a close relationship.

Although I wondered during that unhappy time of my life whether God could ever forgive me for the horrible things I'd done, I know now that He has. As Psalm 40:2 says, "He lifted me out of the slimy pit, out of the mud and mire; he set my feet on a rock"—Jesus. With God, we can bounce back—even from being a child abuser.

KATHY COLLARD MILLER lives in Placentia, California, with her husband Larry and two children. She is the author of nineteen books and is compiler-editor of the best-selling *God's Vitamin C for the Spirit.* Kathy has appeared on many television and radio programs, including *The 700 Club.* She is on the staff of CLASS (Christian Leaders, Authors and Speakers Seminars), Inc., and is a frequent speaker at women's retreats, conferences and church events nationally and internationally.

A Little Red Dot of Faith

Adell Harvey

*I*n 1964 we left our careers in Peoria, Illinois, sold our house and headed for the Endless Mountains of northern Pennsylvania to pastor a mission church in one of John F. Kennedy's Appalachian "poverty pockets." We soon settled into a way of life we loved, ministering to the mountain people and being ministered to by their openness and acceptance.

Then tragedy struck. The rigors of wood-chopping, snow shoveling and rural mission work took their toll on my husband Bill. He suffered a series of heart attacks, followed by a near-fatal stroke, and the doctors recommended open-heart surgery.

We spent a happy Christmas with our three children, then left the next day for Philadelphia.

My mom came to stay in the parsonage with the
kids while Bill and I spent the next six weeks in
the University of Pennsylvania Hospital waiting
for the doctors to get Bill's heart in shape for the
operation.

Bill and I grew very close during those weeks of
"exile," making plans toward the day his heart
would be healthy again and we could renew our
missionary activities. But our plans were not
God's plan. Bill died three days after the surgery,
leaving me to raise ten-year-old Bill Jr., nine-year-
old Mari and toddler Jeff alone.

My immediate problem was how to tell the kids
their daddy had died. Mari, especially, had held
out great hopes that "God's going to make you
well, Daddy."

Before leaving Philadelphia, I phoned Mom with
the sad news and left it to her to break it gently to
the kids. She said Billy sobbed and sobbed, but
Mari just grew very quiet and went into her bedroom. A few minutes later, she came out, her face
radiant.

"I prayed that God would make Daddy well,"
she said, "and He did. Daddy's well forever now
and will never be sick again."

We planned a memorial service for Bill at our
little church in the Endless Mountains, greeted
dozens of visitors who dropped by to pay their re-
spects and packed like crazy for the long trip back
to Illinois. Vacating the parsonage for the next
pastor's family, we had to determine what to take
with us and what to discard.

We packed Mergatroid, our beat-up Chevy van, to the hilt, loaded in the kids, and then Mom and I climbed into the front seats. We had 1,500 miles to travel in two days in order to arrive in Peoria in time for Bill's funeral there.

A driver I wasn't. Bill had always done most of the driving, and for me, even twenty miles was a major trip. I was so thankful Mom was along as my copilot. She didn't drive, but she sure knew how to read road signs. I was also thankful for what must have been a legion of guardian angels God sent to keep that van on the road. A terrific blizzard swept across the Great Lakes area that day, threatening to sweep us off the highway.

That night when we stopped at a motel, Mom had to unclench my fingers one by one from the steering wheel, ease me out of the driver's seat and massage my back so I could stand erect. My back muscles were so taut she could have played a Gypsy serenade on them.

We finally reached the Illinois border just in time for the worst road conditions that area had ever seen. Visibility was zero as the winds picked up the rich black dirt which made Illinois farming famous and swirled it into the snow. When the state police closed the highway, we joined hundreds of other stranded travelers squeezed into a Stuckey's Travel Stop to wait out the storm.

Bill's viewing was scheduled for that evening, and there we were, stranded two hours' drive from home. A kindly trucker, hearing of our plight, made an offer we couldn't refuse. "I've got to try to get through tonight myself. If you'll just trust me and stay close, I'll lead you."

That night I learned what faith is all about. For mile after mile we couldn't see a thing but the tiny red dot of the truck's one bright tail light. There was no way to tell if the driver was taking wrong turns, heading for a ditch or leading us into a farmer's backyard. I just had to follow that red dot and trust.

We made it home in time for the viewing and buried Bill the next day, my thirtieth birthday. I entered the fearful world of widowhood and learned to follow that "little red dot" of faith through many dark and trying situations.

I bought an old farmhouse across the lane from Mom's house, unconsciously seeking the "security blanket" of home. The charming old farmhouse presented a few problems, however, for someone as unmechanical as I am. Little things like blown fuses sent me into a tailspin. Even changing light bulbs taxed my abilities. And hanging storm windows? That stunt nearly cost me my life, my faith and my mind.

Determined to get the blamed things up on the old two-story farmhouse, I wrestled with a rickety ladder, then climbed up to the first window, lugging a heavy storm sash along. It didn't fit. The hooker-doodle things wouldn't go over the hooks.

I struggled harder, but the ladder slipped; I and

a heavy storm window crashed to the ground. Sprawled among bits of shattered glass and disheveled marigolds, for the first time in my life I actually swore.

I raved at God, "If you hadn't taken my husband none of this would have happened. We were faithfully serving You, and look how You repaid us! This whole thing is *Your* fault!"

Never before or since have I been so angry, so completely out of control. I screamed, I stomped, I raged. The kids thought surely I had landed on my head and lost my mind. They stood by helplessly as I ran inside and flung myself across my bed, sobbing and shouting hysterically.

When my lungs and vocal cords finally played out, I was reduced to a sweat-and-tear-soaked heap of self-pity, lying motionless on the bed.

Then, as I lay there in frustration, I felt someone affectionately stroking my back. But there was no one in sight. It seemed God Himself had come down to comfort me. He patted my back tenderly and gently, as if to say, *It's all right, Little One— now that you've got all that out of your system, let's get back on speaking terms.*

Actually, it has taken awhile for us to get back on speaking terms. But whenever I start feeling sorry for myself or getting angry again, I think back to the night when I had nothing to follow through the fog but a little red dot. If I could have faith *that* night, I should be able to have it now. Thank you, God, for giving me back that little red dot of faith!

ADELL HARVEY says her main claim to fame is that she raised eight children to reasonably normal adulthood and managed to get every one of them housebroken. All eight attended Christian colleges and love the Lord. Adell is also the author of ten published books. She lives in Turlock, California, and is in demand as a humorous and inspirational speaker.

Crisis on the Mountain

Carol L. Fitzpatrick

The saucer sled carrying my two-year-old daughter and me careened down the ice-covered mountain. Suddenly the slick, uneven surface propelled the red metal disc high into the air; then, like a discarded, unwanted toy, the disc crashed back again upon the frozen earth. A panic prayer escaped my lips: "God, help me! My back is broken!"

I stretched out one hand, flipped my daughter onto her stomach, then pushed her off the sled to brake her slide and to provide a slow descent for her down the remainder of the slope. Once my own momentum slowed, I leaned from the waist, keeping my back straight and allowed my injured body to fall gently onto the snow. My six years of nurses' aid training seemed to kick in automatically.

"Don't move me—get help!" I shouted to those who rushed to my aid. "Get my daughter! She slid down the mountain," I added. Each breath was agonizing, as if a knife were ripping through my back.

They found my daughter safe and sound, thank God! But for me, the ordeal was only beginning.

Minutes clicked by in slow motion as I lay shivering on the frozen ground, waiting for the ambulance. My mind drifted to earlier that day, a tear-filled morning when I woke up crying and continued to cry sporadically all morning. My husband and three small children tried to coax me out of it with sweet words. The children were excited about the outing we had planned, and one of them said, "Don't cry, Mommy. Come to the mountains and we'll have fun in the snow."

The ambulance finally arrived and took me to a local emergency hospital. Within an hour, X-rays confirmed what I'd expected: a compression fracture of one vertebra just above my shoulder blades. But I would have to be transported down off the mountain to a hospital more equipped to handle orthopedic injuries.

With each descending mile in the ambulance, the pain became more excruciating. I tried to get my mind off it by focusing on why I had cried so uncontrollably that morning. Suddenly I realized what it was: It was the *anniversary*, of course—the anniversary of my father's death.

Christmas had passed and, with the help of a grief counselor, I had finally begun to release my carefully stored anguish over the father I'd lost at this holiday season ten years before. He'd been an alcoholic, and because he died suddenly from a heart attack, there had been no time for resolution or sorely needed apologies.

I was nineteen at the time. An officious, possibly well-meaning but not very tactful neighbor had told me bluntly: "Your father is dead, and there's nothing you can do to change that. Now don't cry and upset your younger siblings." For years I bottled up the anger and the frustration and the grief inside; only recently had I been able to take small steps to release them. Today the tears had flowed freely.

My hospital roommate was a young Christian woman who had been injured in a skiing accident. She took her injury in stride and many encouraging friends visited her. As they spoke of God's love and mercy, I silently seethed at God for adding this latest disaster to the list of crimes He'd committed against me.

I fumed, knowing that young girl didn't have to go home and face months of recovery while caring for three small children. I wondered how I would ever manage!

Nine days later, I left the hospital with a steel back brace to support my body but nothing to bolster my fears. How much mobility would return? And how could I supervise an active two-year-old from the hospital bed my husband had rented for me and moved into the den?

Pain and panic filled my first night home as I slept alone in the den, away from my familiar bedroom. This would be it for months to come! The doctor predicted a nine-month recovery period—

the time it takes a baby to be ready to be born. I
didn't realize then that the Lord was providing the
atmosphere for my *spiritual* rebirth.

In a word, my life now meant *adjustment.* And
when one has nowhere to look but up, one has
time to pause and reflect. *Why has God allowed this?*
my mind begged to understand.

My husband placed our three-year-old in a day-
care center near his office, while our four-year-old
divided his time between preschool and doing his
best to help me. Our two-year-old spent most of
her days sitting in bed with me—mesmerized by
the television in my room.

All seemed to be progressing well until the
four-year-old, in a span of four months, brought
home measles, mumps, chicken pox and strep
throat. Finally his immune system gave out, re-
quiring thirteen weeks of gamma globulin injec-
tions.

By this time my anger level had reached a maxi-
mum. How did God expect me to get through the
first crisis, let alone all the others He was heaping
daily on our family?

At this point my life began to move in a positive
direction. Whereas one self-absorbed neighbor
had mistakenly admonished me to stow my grief
at that crucial time of my father's death, the Lord
now used another neighbor, my friend Cheryl, to
rescue my soul from turmoil. Cheryl had one
small child, yet she readily volunteered to "do
anything" I needed to have done. And no matter
how long the "list" was, she never complained.

She constantly reassured me that Jesus loved me. Although I never doubted her sincerity, the concepts of suffering and love just didn't appear compatible to me.

When Cheryl invited me to attend a Bible study with her, I stifled the urge to expound again on why it was obvious God didn't care about me. I just said, "No." Again she asked, and again I said, "No."

The third time I told Cheryl no, something stirred within me. *What if it actually helps?* I considered. But a mental image of those strange women staring at my back brace changed my mind again. Finally I called a place I had seen advertised as "Dial-a-Prayer." After I poured out my needs to this stranger, it somehow made sense to call Cheryl back. *What if Cheryl's friends are kind like the one who just prayed with me?* I thought. And if they weren't—no problem. I could claim excruciating pain and Cheryl would bring me home. Besides, the offer of a free baby sitter for several hours was too good to pass up.

The women extended a cordial greeting and also expressed genuine interest in knowing me. This sense of acceptance began to melt the iceberg in my spirit. The leader began the study.

What *really* got my attention was a verse she read: "Therefore I tell you that no one who is speaking by the Spirit of God says, 'Jesus be cursed,' and no one can say, 'Jesus is Lord,' except by the Holy Spirit" (1 Corinthians 12:3). Whatever she said after that is but a blur, for God's Word had just ripped my heart wide open.

This phrase struck me because I had cursed God continually since the time my father died, furious that there was no way to fix my pain. Two years after his death we also lost our first child, and I continued to hold onto and nurse my anger at God as if it were a prized possession. Hope was a foreign language to me, totally unintelligible.

One day, while flipping through TV channels, I saw Corrie ten Boom. Her testimony told of how God called her to forgive the prison guard who was responsible for the death of her sister. *What a disarming thought*, I mused, *but how could she forgive him?*

Later that week, Billy Graham's televised crusade beckoned to me; I remember touching the screen as though reaching out to grasp the forgiveness God dispensed.

On Father's Day, 1973, I committed my soul and what remained of the use of my body to my Father in heaven. Once my heart, mind and soul were set free, the Lord and my Bible became my constant companions. I read the Word hungrily, seeking and finding answers to every question and reservation I had concerning God. Gradually the feelings of abandonment and anger left and were replaced with wholeness.

That August I taught Vacation Bible School on my front lawn for all the neighborhood children. Each of my children and many of the neighbor children accepted the Lord. It took another thirteen years for my husband to see his spiritual need, but the children and I bolstered one another as we grew in our faith.

During the past twenty-three years, I've never gone without extensive Bible study and prayer as I continually seek His will for my life. And the Lord has remained faithful, both in showing me how to get through the stages of grief without getting stuck forever in the one called anger, and in proving to me that He "will never leave me or forsake me."

CAROL L. FITZPATRICK is married and the mother of three grown children. She and her husband reside in Lake Forest, California. Carol has been a Vacation Bible School teacher, Bible study leader, Precept Ministries leader and was co-director of the Orange County Christian Writers Fellowship from 1993 to 1995. Carol is a graduate of CLASS (Christian Leaders, Authors and Speakers Seminars), Inc. She is a speaker and the author of six books, the first of which was *A Time to Grieve*, published in 1995.

CHAPTER 3

BOUNCE BACK FROM REGRET

*I*n order to attain peace of heart and mind, it is necessary to put our past failures and mistakes behind us. After we confess to God and repent, we must accept His forgiveness, forgive ourselves and move on. In this chapter, the writers tell how they were finally able to do this through prayer or through regular study and application of the Scriptures to their lives.

> . . . *I will forgive their wickedness and will remember their sins no more. (Jeremiah 31:34)*

The Last Walk

Laura Sabin Riley

The call came unexpectedly late one evening. As I listened to the voice on the other end tears began to pool in my eyes and a wave of guilt washed over me. "Ok, Dad, I understand. I'll be there as soon as I can," was the only reply I could squeak out. A few more details and the conversation ended. I hung up the phone and, no longer needing to restrain myself, I began to weep, softly at first and then harder as I felt my husband's arms slip around me.

"What is it, Laura? What's wrong? Who was that on the phone?" my husband asked, panic in his voice.

I managed to explain between sobs. "It was my dad. . . . It's my grandma. She's in the hospital with pneumonia and the doctors don't think she's going to make it." I looked up into my husband's eyes for reassurance.

"Well, you need to get on a plane and go see her right away," he instructed.

"I know," I responded, panic now rising in my voice, "but what do you say to someone you have not seen in fifteen years?"

Another pang of guilt jabbed at me. I had let so much time pass between my grandparents and me. I searched my memory for remnants from my last visit with them—the summer I was sixteen years old. But nothing came to me. The thousands of miles that separated us no longer seemed like justification for not visiting, nor did the fact that college, then marriage, children and life in general had kept me "too busy." Suddenly everything I had spent the last fifteen years doing didn't seem so important anymore.

I felt ashamed. How could I face her now? *Maybe I shouldn't go*, I thought. *She probably thinks I don't even care about her.* A restlessness inside told me I was wrong on both counts. This time nothing else seemed as important as seeing Grandma again.

On the plane I closed my eyes and tried to re-member the little whitewashed house with the brick steps where my grandparents still lived. I could picture the lush green yard where my brothers and I used to run and play during sum-mer vacations. I saw the pink blossoms on the cherry trees that dotted their property and thought I could even smell Grandma's mouth-wa-tering cherry pies baking in the oven. Grandma's kitchen was one of my favorite places.

There was something else I loved about going to Grandma's—what was it? It was something we did together, but I couldn't remember.

The pilot's voice on the intercom announcing our descent into Des Moines shattered my thoughts, and the hope of any more recollection was lost in the drone of the engines. I sighed wearily and began to collect my things.

My legs felt like lead as I stepped from the car and entered the front doors of the hospital. The faint smell of death curled at my nose, and I shook my head, refusing to acknowledge it. As we made the trek down the long corridors to Grandma's hospital room I began to pray, *Lord, I need You to help me right now. I feel so weak. I don't know what to say to Grandma. I don't even know if she'll remember me. Somehow, Lord, I need to let her know that I love her—that I have always loved her, even in my absence. Please give me the words.*

As I finished my prayer, I found myself standing outside the door to Grandma's room. I stood there for a few moments, watching the steady rise and fall of her chest. She was so thin I could see her heart beating through her hospital gown. As I lingered in the doorway I heard a voice whisper to me, *You don't need to say anything. Your being here is enough. She has been waiting for you.* Though it was an inner voice, the words were real, very real.

I found new courage from those words that stirred in my heart, and I took a few steps into the room. Grandma's head turned toward the doorway and a faint smile appeared on her lips. "There you are," she said, extending a hand, "I've been waiting for you."

Smiling back, I took her hand and seated myself on the edge of her bed, gazing into her soft hazel eyes. She was just as I had remembered, only more frail. She looked very tired.

As I bent to hug her, I began to cry softly. But the tears were no longer those of fear or guilt; they were tears of joy, the kind you cry when you see an old friend after a very long time, and she was sharing them with me.

After awhile we dried our eyes and began to talk. She seemed to be filled with a new energy as she spoke of years past and my childhood visits. There was a softness in her words as she spoke, a sweetness in her eyes as she gazed up at me, and I realized that she harbored no ill feelings toward my absence the past fifteen years. She had only feelings of joy in my presence.

We spent the next few days that way, I at her bedside and she recounting years past. Although I felt at peace being there with her, something was still troubling me. It was a memory lingering behind a closed door that I couldn't get open.

On the last day of my visit she patted my hand and, looking out the window, said, "Remember our walks?"

Our walks! The words sprung at me and something inside my head clicked as a door from the past flew open. "Oh yes," I began excitedly as the memory became clearer, "we used to go for walks every night after supper!"

Her eyes seemed to sparkle as she recalled, "I loved those walks with you. We'd pick wildflowers and look for squirrels and talk about anything that was on our hearts."

Yes, now I remembered. Grandma loved to walk. She walked with Grandpa unless I was there; then she walked with me. Down by the riverbank, through the park, along the sleepy town's streets at dusk; Grandma walked everywhere I wanted to go. Those walks were special to both of us.

The look in her eyes told me she wished she could get up now and take one last walk with me, but the memories would have to do. She sighed deeply and, wrapping her arms around me, gave me one last hug. Neither one of us said it, but we both knew it would be the last.

A few weeks later I got the call that Grandma had passed away. I listened intently as my mother told me that Grandma's last words to the nurse had been that she was going for a walk with Jesus. As I hung up the phone this time, I didn't cry. Instead a smile crept over me as I thought of Grandma. *Looks like she got to take that last walk after all.*

LAURA SABIN RILEY is a freelance writer, wife and mother. Her short stories and articles have been published in various Christian publications, and she is currently in the process of writing a devotional book for stay-at-home moms. In addition, she is active in the drama and women's ministries at her church. Laura lives in Yuma, Arizona.

Faithquake!

John-Eva B. Orsa

I was the "Christian" in the family—or so I pridefully believed until Christmas morning, 1987. That's when my "Miracle on Charles Street" occurred.

Much like the mother in the classic "Miracle on 34th Street," my belief system was about to be severely shaken. I affectionately refer to it now as a faithquake, which both the movie mom and I experienced.

As the movie plot unfolds, we see a woman whose take-charge, in-control appearance is only a tough cover-up for a broken heart. Her shattered faith is being passed along to her young daughter who is developing a hard heart of her own. Their beliefs are shaken when Santa Claus shows up. When, in a trial, he proves that he is real, he wins over their hearts and "they all live happily ever after."

In my case, I believed my broken heart and shattered faith were somebody else's fault. For years I had been wearing a set of wedding rings with the diamond missing. It had fallen out, and when people noticed, they would typically say, "You should get that replaced."

"Never!" I would defiantly reply, leaving the explanation to their imagination. For me, the ring with the missing diamond was the symbol of what our marriage had become. It looked good from a distance until you got up close and saw how empty it really was.

My husband had found the diamond and, thinking it was just a piece of glass, tossed it away. My response had been, "How appropriate!" Something I had cherished, handled with such indifference. One more callous act to chip away at the fragile foundation of our marriage.

That foundation had some major cracks from the very beginning. When it started, I was eighteen and pregnant. My "knight in shining armor" was not quite twenty and was about to leave for Vietnam. When he returned one year later, he looked much the same, but he brought with him an invisible wall that kept everyone, including me, from getting close enough to see how empty he felt inside.

The effect of that war on my husband did not get addressed until some sixteen years after the fact. By then, a fault line the size of the San Andreas was running smack dab through the middle of our marriage. Crazy as it sounds, we'd learned to live with it, each of us assuming it was the other's fault. We filled our lives with busyness and no one knew how hollow and empty we were.

Psalm 51 had become a place of frequent solace for my troubled soul, but it was a psalm I just read—not understood.

Now Christmas morning was upon us, and a faithquake was about to hit Charles Street. Just what was needed for knocking down walls and destroying faulty foundations.

Our son, who was twenty years old at the time, said, "Mom, I got you something special! I want you to open it first." How miraculously his precious gift would prepare the way for his father's gift. My favorite gifts from him had always been handprints on construction paper, but this one definitely became a contender for first place. It was a beautiful ring with a cluster of fifteen small diamonds. What a sacrifice it must have been for him on his meager salary! It should have melted any hardened heart.

But, as my husband timidly approached me with his gift, I looked him squarely in the eye and said, "I don't want that."

What he said next shook me right out of my firm resolve: "God told me to buy you this," he said. He went on to explain that, a few days earlier, he had been at a department store with a friend who was buying a gift at the jewelry counter. While he was standing there, he casually looked down and heard God speak directly to him.

I'm ashamed to admit it, but I was self-righteously wondering, *So when did You start speaking to heathens, God?* By His grace, I was too dumbfounded to say a word.

I opened the small velvet box. It was a gift that seemed to me to be straight from heaven! It was an exquisite gold wedding band with a silver cross etched in the center, surrounded by a ring of diamonds. As I looked around at the apprehensive faces of my family, it was as if I heard God say, *Keep* Me *at the center of your life and I shall surround you with diamonds of blessings.*

I started to tremble and a flood of tears blinded me temporarily. As the faithquake subsided, the Son rose again to the position where He belonged in my life. He showed me my psalm of solace as it was meant to be seen; as a psalm of *repentance*.

I received the most incredible gifts of the heart that Christmas morning and, amazingly, found one of my own to give. It was right there in Psalm 51:15-17: "O Lord, open my lips, and my mouth will declare your praise. You do not delight in sacrifice, or I would bring it; you do not take pleasure in burnt offerings. The sacrifices of God are a broken spirit; a broken and contrite heart, O God, you will not despise."

JOHN-EVA B. ORSA enjoys teaching and writing women's Bible studies. She always hopes these studies will encourage women and reveal the truth of God's love for them. John-Eva and her family live in Moorpark, California, where she is currently working on a book with the proposed title, *Earthquakes and Unloved Wives: The Things That Make the Earth Shake.*

Out of the Mouths of Babes

J.J. Jenkins

I hung up the phone. I felt like I was moving in slow motion. Panic began to take over my mind. How could I have said yes? Had I completely lost my mind?

I knew perfectly well that my husband's birthday celebration was planned for tomorrow, and yet I had said, "Yes, sure, I'll make my special potato candy for the bake sale."

I felt obligated to say yes. This was the Christian preschool's big fund-raising carnival and I didn't want to let my son or the school down. Actually, I could have stopped with making something for the bake sale booth, but no, I always had to go too far.

The next words out of my mouth were, "Of course, I'd be glad to work in one of the booths at the carnival tomorrow."

That was my voice saying those words on the phone—the words just slipped right out of my mouth—but *why*?

Maybe it was confusion from the pressure of knowing that my "white-gloved" mother-in-law and her husband would be here in my house in less than thirty-six hours that caused my brain to malfunction and my mouth to say "yes" when it should have said "no."

"Not for dinner, dear," my mother-in-law said, "but we *could* have dessert with all of you. I'm sure you'll be fixing something wonderful!"

This meant I would have to create a fabulous homemade birthday cake, naturally from scratch. Now, after my overgenerous volunteering, there would certainly be no time for creative genius and probably not even time for a box of Betty Crocker cake mix.

I felt all the color drain out of my face as I began to realize what an awful mistake I had made. My mind floundered, shifted into passing gear and rummaged frantically for an idea. I sent up a distraught prayer:

"Oh dear Lord, what can I do?"

Suddenly, like a neon light, the words "ice cream mold" flashed across my brain. Aha! Ice cream frozen in a pretty shape—that would be unique. I had never heard of an ice cream mold before, but it seemed to be an answer to my prayer, and it sounded like a time-saving, face-saving great idea. An ice cream mold with a store-bought cake—that would do nicely!

After locating my Tupperware mold, Little John and I dashed to the store to get everything needed for the potato candy and, most importantly, the ice cream for tomorrow night's birthday celebration.

The next morning was a whirlwind of activity as I raced against the clock to get the house tidied and everything ready for the big day. Then I ran next door to borrow our neighbor's young daughter Liz, who was going to babysit Little John at the carnival while I was selling baked goods in the booth.

The carnival was already underway when we arrived. Liz and Little John took off to enjoy the games and rides and I headed for my booth. During the day, while fulfilling my duties, my thoughts jumped ahead, anxiously going over each detail. *Had I forgotten anything? Napkins—ok. Coffee —ok . . .*

"How much are those chocolate cookies?" The little girl's voice came from somewhere below my counter, jerking me back to the present.

I answered her question and sold her a cookie. I glanced at my watch. Only thirty minutes and my shift would be finished. Thank goodness!

This was the first time all day I had been aware of the smell of the popcorn and the racket of the popper in the booth next to me. Looking across the blacktop, I saw my son with Liz. I felt a twinge and wished it were me showing Little John the sights of the carnival. I appreciated Liz coming to take care of him while I was in the booth, but deep inside, I felt I was missing out on something very special.

"Mrs. Waters . . ." I recognized Mrs. Wells's voice and turned from my selling duties. "Could you possibly work the booth for one more hour? Sue Ann got sick on the Ferris wheel and her mother had to take her home." Her words sounded out of breath.

"I . . . I . . . I can't! It's my husband's birthday and my in-laws are coming over." I finally got the words out.

"Well, if you could stay just a half hour more, then maybe I can get Marianne to help," Mrs. Wells pleaded.

"Ok, half an hour, but that's it," I said to the back of her head. She had turned to go as soon as my "ok" had been uttered.

The time went fast because the booth had gotten very busy. At last my replacement showed up and I was free. I was able to get Liz and Little John ready to go and into the car in a matter of minutes. We headed for home.

I dashed through the door with my arms loaded with stuff from the car. Liz had already gone home and I had told Little John he could play in the backyard. I hurried to the freezer to pull out my glorious ice cream mold. I knew this fabulous dessert would save the day!

I had packed the ice cream into the mold the night before and tucked it safely away in the freezer. As I pulled it out, I noticed it was much harder than I had thought it would be.

"Mommy," Little John's voice called to me as he rounded the corner of the kitchen.

"Not now, Little John. Mommy's busy. Go back outside and play," I said as I carried my rock-hard mold to the counter. I could almost hear the clock ticking. I pounded! I prodded! I prayed! But the ice cream wouldn't budge. Through this whole process my preschooler had been tugging at my leg, trying desperately to get my attention. Three times I had successfully shooed him out the door to play. But he had been separated from me most of the day and part of yesterday, so this time he was not going to move. He wanted my attention and he was going to have his say.

One more tug on my leg from the persistent preschooler and all the frustrations from my day came pouring out.

"Don't you know I don't have time for this! Can't you see I'm busy? I have to get this ice cream ready before your dad gets home and it's stuck in this stupid mold!" My words came spewing out.

My brave little one held his ground. He looked up at me with tear-filled eyes, took a big breath and said, "*People* are more important than ice cream!"

I was stunned. Little John's words pierced my heart. I broke into tears, reached down, scooped up my son and held him tight.

I have never forgotten the lesson I learned that day from my tiny teacher. In the confusion of trying to be the perfect mother, perfect wife and perfect daughter-in-law, I had lost sight of what was really important. I don't usually hear God speaking aloud to me, and yet that day the words of wisdom that came from my little boy were definitely *heaven-sent*.

My son is now twenty-eight and it seems a lifetime since that day in the kitchen. I still have a knack for getting myself inundated with work, real or self-imposed. It's still easy for me to lose sight of the truly important things in life. It's at those times when my son's words come back to me: "People *are* more important than ice cream!"

J.J. JENKINS was a wife and homemaker for fifteen years before returning to college and earning a certificate in sign language. She joined the ranks of "working single moms," serving as an instructional aide in the Deaf and Hard of Hearing Program in a southern California high school. With her two children now grown, she has recently returned to college again, working toward becoming a speech therapist. J.J. is an avid reader and loves to write. She has written poetry, newsletters, humorous stories and term papers and has filled mountains of notebooks with her journaling. She is optimistic that one of these days the best of all this writing will become her book.

Out of the Pit

Susan Titus Osborn

Staring out of my hotel window on that winter's day in Washington, DC, I watched huge chunks of ice drift lazily down the Potomac River. I rubbed my arms and shivered—partly from the cold, but mostly from the memory forming in my mind.

I recalled the morning my husband, looking tired and tense, walked into the kitchen, sat down at the table and said, "I care about you, but I don't love you enough to live with you anymore."

After twenty-two years of marriage, my world crumbled around me. I had realized things weren't right between us, but I didn't dream that he wanted out of our marriage. We had been going to a Christian counselor for six months, but to no avail. The marriage was dead, and a part of me died with it because so much of my life revolved around my husband.

Going through a divorce was the most painful

ordeal I have ever experienced. I met my husband
at seventeen and fell in love. We were married
four years later, and we were happy for about fifteen years. With the addition of two children, our
family life flowed smoothly like the Potomac
River on a warm, summer day.

Then problems arose—easily solved at first, but
more difficult to solve later on. I built an icy wall
of insulation around myself to keep from feeling
the pain. As time passed, I became numb from the
cold. I forgot how to love; I forgot how to live.
The course of my life became filled with chunks
of ice like the Potomac River on a cold winter day.

Emotionally, I had been in a deep pit. I was too
stressed to pray and too fragmented to read the
Bible. It was impossible for me to reach out and
call on God during that period when I needed
Him most. God seemed distant and silent.

I wanted my situation to be changed, my problems solved, although I was unwilling or unable to
do anything to alter my circumstances. There
were times when I didn't want to face the future—the next day, the next week, the next year. I
didn't have the strength to turn to God.

The uncertainty of what might happen scared
me. I didn't know if I would be able to support
myself and my two sons as a freelance writer. Because I didn't have a college degree, I didn't know
what else I could do to earn a living. I hadn't
worked full time in nineteen years. Plus I had college expenses to pay: my son Rich was attending
the University of California at Santa Barbara, and

I was working toward my BA degree part time. My other son Mike was a senior in high school.

At the time of the divorce, my mental attitude had a negative effect on my sons. They too suffered from the divorce. Yet I didn't have the spiritual reserves to comfort them or quell their doubts and fears.

I wanted instantaneous changes. God's timing, however, was not my timing. One step at a time, I began to climb out of the pit, but it was not easy. Many times I lost my footing and slipped backward. My forward motion often seemed one inch at a time.

Eventually I realized that God had been there all along, waiting for me to reach out and take His hand. Although He didn't lift me out of the pit, I could sense His presence as I slowly made the climb.

In time, I was able to pray again and to listen for His answer. I now realize God was there in spite of my attitude—always helping me through the next five minutes, the next hour, the next day.

As I compared the river with the last time I had seen it, one summer several years before, I saw a remarkable contrast! In the summer, boats charted a course up and down the river, bringing tourists and cargo. Children fished and played on the river's wide banks. Geese, ducks and herons dipped into the river to find food.

Today in the cold stillness below me, I saw no boats, no children and no waterfowl. Huge chunks of ice impeded the flow of the mighty Potomac. Just like the river, I knew I could only be an effective vessel for the Lord if my ice-encrusted heart was melted.

I cried out, "Lord, I never dreamed the death of my marriage would be so painful. I don't ever want to be hurt like this again." I felt as useless as the cold river below me.

I stood at that window, lost in thought, for a long time. As winter passed, the sun would again warm the river and bring it back to life. The boats, the children and the waterfowl would return.

Now, ten years later, I look back and understand. I never dreamed my life would take the path it has. When I had nothing but a thread linking me to God, I learned to step out in faith and take risks. If I had not been forced to earn a living, I would never have developed my current programs and ministries. After being a single parent for six years, I am now blessed with a supportive husband and a thriving business.

I needed to let go of the icy wall in my heart. To help others, I needed to be able to empathize with them. To love others, I had to become vulnerable once more. I realized I could not have accomplished these goals in my own strength.

Loving too much leaves us open to the danger of being hurt, but loving too little can cause us to forget how to love and how to live. It was only when I was ready to allow God to warm me, to melt the ice in my heart, that He was ready to work in my life again.

Adapted from stories that first appeared in *Rest Stops for Single Mothers,* authored by Susan Titus Osborn and Lucille Moses, published by Broadman & Holman Publishers 1995. Used with permission.

SUSAN TITUS OSBORN is editor of *The Christian Communicator.* She is also an adjunct professor at Pacific Christian College in Fullerton, California. She has authored twelve books and numerous articles, devotionals and curriculum materials. Susan is a publisher's representative and teaches at writers' conferences across the U.S. and internationally.

CHAPTER 4

BOUNCE BACK FROM GRIEF

or some people, the wrenching sense of loss when a loved one dies is so overwhelming that life loses its meaning and nothing matters to them anymore. When this happens, we have three choices: We can choose to stay stuck in our pain, we can choose to deny and hide from it or we can turn it over to God and let Him be with us as we "walk through the valley of the shadow of death." The stories in this chapter show how that third choice, in every case, was the choice that healed the pain.

Blessed are those who mourn, for they will be comforted. (Matthew 5:4)

Disappointed with God

Marilyn Willett Heavilin

When we get the full picture of God—the picture that includes the awesome and the fearsome traits—then we aren't quite so surprised by the things that come into our lives. I have seen, through my experiences of the deaths of three of my children, the compassion God has shown to me and His willingness to interact with me. He has helped me and has been patient with me as I have struggled to learn more about Him and His ways.

Jimmy died of crib death when he was seven weeks old in 1964; a year and a half later we had identical twin boys, born on Christmas morning. Ten days later one of them died. When Ethan died, the second child within a year and a half, I was very angry. I was just plain mad at God. This wasn't fair; I didn't understand it. I asked God, *If You were going to take him away, why did You give me twins in the first place?*

As I stood there and watched that little guy struggle for every breath, I felt God was saying to me, *Marilyn, I loved you enough to die for you. Do you love Me enough to trust Me with this child?* I sat on the floor in the bathroom of the private room the hospital had given us and I argued with God. After I had spoken my piece, I finally said, *I'm not going to argue anymore. I give You control of this little baby. But just remember, I still don't like it!* I believe God allowed Ethan to live until I could say I would accept His will. How thankful I am He knew me well enough to give me some time. I believe my struggle would have been so much harder if I had still been arguing with Him about it when my baby died.

We see in Scripture God even gave Jesus Christ time. When Jesus was faced with His own death, God, in effect, let Him come back and say, "Are You sure? Is that what we have to do? Do we really have to go through that?"

Scripture says, "Going a little farther, he fell with his face to the ground and prayed, 'My Father, if it is possible, may this cup be taken from me. Yet not as I will, but as you will' " (Matthew 26:39).

I too asked God, "Do You know what You're doing? Are You really sure? Isn't there any other way?" But God allowed me to reach the point where I could say, "Ok. Whatever it is, I will accept it. I don't like it, but I'm willing to work with it."

I still had anger and I still had difficulties to

work with, but I was not a bitter woman. I am so thankful the bitterness was gone before Ethan died. I was still on speaking terms with God, and He could work with me as we moved along.

My third child to die was Nathan, seventeen years after his twin brother Ethan had died. Nathan was killed by a drunk driver. It was all over before I ever really got to talk to God. The answer was just simply, *No. He's not going to live. He's going to die.* You see, this time, I was already at the point where I could say, "I don't understand it, but I trust You."

This statement has been attributed to Charles Spurgeon: "God is too good to be unkind; too wise to be mistaken. . . . When you cannot trace His hand, you can always trust His heart."

When my sons died, at times my heart was so sick I could not pray, even though I had a very consistent prayer life and quiet time prior to their deaths. The longest sentence I could utter was, "Lord, help me." Trauma causes us to be unable to concentrate on any one thing longer than a few seconds, and that inability to focus enters into our spiritual life as well as our physical life.

However, I also realize I was disappointed with God. I remember a close family member who stated repeatedly after Nate's death, "I never thought God would do this." While I didn't say those words aloud, I certainly agreed with the thought. When I tried to pray, a multitude of emotions so overwhelmed me that I could not pray. No words would come.

My particular approach was to keep trying until
I was able to read a full sentence from the Bible
and understand it, until I was able to utter at least
a few words in prayer before I melted into a pud-
dle of tears. Yet, for some, the disappointment
they feel within themselves toward God has become a barrier between them and God, and they
have quit trying to pray.

Can you relate to that? Are you disappointed
with God? Perhaps you need to do as the psalmist
did and admit your disappointment with God. He
can handle it. He wants to hear from you!

Listen to some of the statements from Psalms. I
know I can often identify with these and I'm sure
you can too.

> I cry to the Lord; I call and call to him.
> Oh, that he would listen. I am in deep
> trouble and I need his help so badly. All
> night long I pray, lifting my hands to
> heaven, pleading. There can be no joy for
> me until he acts. I think of God and moan,
> overwhelmed with longing for his help. I
> cannot sleep until you act. I am too dis-
> tressed even to pray! (Psalm 77:1-4, TLB)

> I weep with grief; my heart is heavy with
> sorrow; encourage and cheer me with your
> words. (Psalm 119:28, TLB)

King David was not afraid to share his frustration and discouragement. Rather than become si-

lent before God, he told the Lord just how he felt. I encourage you to do the same thing. If you're disappointed with God, if you're frustrated, if you're discouraged—say so. He wants to talk with you.

Taken from Chapters 1 and 7, *I'm Listening Lord: Hearing God's Voice When You Pray* by Marilyn Heavilin © 1993 Thomas Nelson Publishers. Used by permission.

MARILYN WILLETT HEAVILIN is a speaker and writer, a wife of thirty-eight years, the mother of five children and the grandmother of four. She and her husband Glen live in Redlands, California. She is author of five best-selling books and an international motivational speaker. She is also a frequent speaker for support groups for bereaved parents and also speaks at writers' conferences, churches, Christian conference centers and universities across the country.

From Grief to Joy

Douglas A. Clark

The grim-faced surgeon followed the stretcher out of the operating theater. On it lay the sedated body of my wife, Ruth. He spoke to me in a subdued voice: "Your wife has terminal cancer."

Wild thoughts raced through my mind. *No, it can't be true. Surely there is some mistake.* The expressions on the faces of nurses and attendants testified mutely that it was true.

There had been no warning signals. We were both familiar with the warning signs of cancer, but hers was ovarian cancer, the silent destroyer. How could this have happened? Swimming, walking, exercising and watching calories were part of her lifestyle. But with ovarian cancer, these didn't count.

It was necessary to leave Australia and bid farewell to the church. We had grown to love our Christian supporters there. Stephen, our Bible

83

translator son, flew down from Papua, New Guinea. Later, our other children, Stanley, Susan and Jonathan, joined us as well.

I was unable to be of much help because of a broken leg, encased in a heavy cast. When we were able to leave Perth, it was in wheelchairs, pushed through the airports by our children. At last we were home in the U.S. and thankful for a safe arrival.

During the next twelve months, Ruth underwent further surgery and painful chemotherapy treatments. Through it all, her faith remained strong, and I never heard her complain or admit to pain, although I knew she must have suffered. Prayers of friends, family and church members were of much encouragement.

However, the healing we had asked for was not to be. God had other plans for His child. During the difficult months our Lord provided comfort, assurance of His love and a peace that surpassed understanding.

Shortly before her death I said, "Ruth, it seems the Lord hasn't answered our prayers for healing."

"But He has," she quickly replied. "I am being healed." I knew what she meant. Her mind was already fixed on her eternal home, where she would have complete healing of body.

When she finally slipped away, my grief was severe. I never admitted to it when friends asked, but had it not been for the grace of the Lord I could not have endured the pain of separation. We had been each other's best friend for the forty-three years of our marriage, serving the Lord together in the ministry. During the years of university teaching we had adjacent offices. We shared a mutual interest in travel and missions.

The period following the funeral was traumatic. It involved disposing of clothing, sitting alone in restaurants at a table for two, watching with envy the happy couples, entering a dark and silent house at night. Yet with it all I knew that I was never alone, for the presence of the Lord sustained me day by day.

I realized that grief was inescapable and that it was often accompanied with feelings of guilt, regret, confusion, loneliness and loss of self-identity. Although grief was inevitable, it was necessary for the healing of soul and spirit. Time was also an ally, and over the months and years the painful memories began to fade.

Most important of all, I found, was the daily strength provided by waiting on the Lord. The Holy Spirit spoke through prayer and the Word. Gradually I began to bounce back from grief.

Some I knew had reacted badly to grief. They exhibited anger and bitterness, blaming the Lord for their losses, accusing God of being unjust. I could never experience this kind of attitude. As a pastor I had often comforted the bereaved, and in my situation I found that peace comes in acceptance of His will. I believed His will was good and perfect in spite of circumstances.

How could I be angry with God? Ruth was released from pain and was now in the Father's house. While God may not answer our prayers the way we would like, He always loves us, and I trusted Him. Ruth, contemplating heaven, had said, "I can hardly wait."

Grief gradually subsided and I faced the question, "What next?" Two options faced me. As a retired widower of seventy, I could settle back and wait for the end of life's journey. Around me I saw others who had become depressed, aimless, rooted before their television sets and so miserable no one enjoyed being near them. Like autumn leaves waiting to fall, they waited for their end.

The other option was returning to the ministry we had shared together. Prior to retirement, we had spent summers in Venezuela, Libya, Panama and Belize as mission volunteers in English-language churches. After retirement we invested five years in Guam, Morocco, Singapore and Australia. But would I still be considered at my age and status as a widower?

I made my decision quickly. I rejected the first option. My health was excellent and I decided to go for it in further ministries if possible. I felt it was what the Lord wanted, what Ruth would have wanted and what I wanted. I would not sit around feeling sorry for myself but watch for the opportunity for me to serve.

I didn't wait long. One night I received a call from a church in Darwin, Australia, where we had served earlier. Then it was back to Guam twice, to Western Australia, once more to Darwin and then to a church on the southern coast of Spain.

In service for the Lord I discovered grief giving way to the rejoicing of the Lord and the truth of the psalm that while "weeping may remain for a night" it follows that "rejoicing comes in the morning" (Psalm 30:5). The psalmist wasn't suggesting that in a twenty-four hour day grief would disappear, but that in God's own time it would be supplanted by His joy.

The writer of Ecclesiastes expressed a similar truth. "There is a time for everything, . . . a time to weep and a time to laugh" (Ecclesiastes 3:1, 4). I discovered it was true, for my sense of humor replaced my feeling of sadness.

There are moments of tender memories of days gone by and a sense of loss that remains. Sometimes tears seem close to the surface. But I have bounced back from sorrow, for the Lord Jesus Christ continues to provide comfort when needed, direction for the future, challenges to meet and fruitfulness in serving Him.

Although I have reached the age of seventy-nine, during the past year I found myself again in Australia for the eighth time, serving with a team in the area of Perth. I completed a four-and-a-half-month interim pastorate at a thriving new church and visited my son in Moscow. I am still looking ahead with a sense of excitement for what the Lord has in store for me. "Wherever He leads I'll go," for "if Jesus goes with me, I'll go anywhere."

God is good, and if there are tears yet to be shed in the remaining years, the promise is "He will wipe every tear" (Revelation 21:4).

A New Yorker by birth, DOUGLAS A. CLARK has enjoyed three related careers in Christian service: pastor, university professor and foreign mission volunteer. He is also involved in writing, which he considers a possible fourth career. Although he retired in 1982, he has continued active in ministry and has held interim pastorates in English-language churches on every continent except Antarctica. Pastor Clark resides in Mesa, Arizona. His family, since the homegoing of his wife, consists of three sons and four grandchildren.

God Gave Me Rainbows

Joyce Althens Minatra

The blue and white Tri-Pacer circled the tiny log house below. From the plane I could see that was the house my son Lee was building for Suzie, his bride-to-be. Suddenly, as the pilot turned the plane to circle again, the wing dipped sharply, and the plane careened, nose first, into the mountainside.

My husband Wayne, my daughter Lori and I were in Alaska for the joyous occasion of Lee's wedding. It was to be a time of celebration and rejoicing, but it suddenly turned into a time of tears and grief. The pilot, Lori and I, though badly injured, miraculously survived. Wayne never regained consciousness. He died ten days later.

The hospital corridor became the "chapel" where loved ones, nurses and I, from my hospital bed, witnessed the marriage of Lee and Suzie.

One month later, Lee and Suzie and Lori returned with me to our New Hampshire home to help me recover from my injuries and prepare for the coming winter. We were comforted by the love and care of God's people as they came alongside in our time of need.

After Christmas Lee and Suzie left to begin their new life in Alaska. Lori stayed and became my guardian angel until she married a year later and left to live in Alaska. Then I was alone to face the emptiness of my heart and my home.

The pain of losing my husband was terrible. My heart hurt, and I couldn't bear to think of the awful emptiness that stretched ahead. I thought I might shatter into a million pieces. I felt fragile and wounded. I spent many lonely nights feeling all but lost.

One such lonely night, sobs tore at my very soul. I wept until there were no more tears and then, finally, I slept. At dawn I awoke to the sound of rain dripping from the eaves. I ran downstairs and flung open the door. There before me was a magical morning of misty air and pine boughs dripping with rain. Birds sang and splashed in puddles made by the rain in the night. I knew this was my personal gift from the Lord. The tears of the night had given way to the joy of the morning.

I began to look for God's gifts when I needed His assurance—a rainbow, a rare pileated woodpecker in the pine trees, a crisp blue-sky day—all of these and more kept my eyes on Him instead of on my grief.

"Joyce, never allow yourself to wallow in self-pity." These wise words of a dear friend came back many times when I was tempted to think "poor me." I found the antidote for self-pity is praise, and it was praise that lifted me out of the mire of self-pity. I prayed that somehow my painful loss would comfort and encourage others— that nothing of this tragedy would be wasted.

Many times I was tempted to pull the covers over my head and just feel sorry for myself. But I made the deliberate choice to get out of bed in the morning and prepare for the day. I would not go to town without makeup, with curlers in my hair or clothed carelessly. I no longer had a husband to please, but I did it for the Lord and to feel good about myself.

I set my place at the table and prepared meals for myself. I realized that widowhood was not necessarily a temporary condition. It could be for a lifetime; therefore I had to begin to live for a contented lifetime of singleness. But it was one day and sometimes one hour at a time, deliberately choosing to keep going. As I learned to live, so I learned to walk with God, discovering a new relationship with Him as Companion, Friend, Protector and yes, Husband and Lover. With Him I discovered who I was as a single woman.

I also discovered that life in New England, with maintenance of home, car and snowy driveways, required more physical energy than I possessed. After much prayer and counsel with godly people, I left my home to live in Hawaii until the Lord directed otherwise. I left behind family and friends

who loved me, but perhaps would not have allowed God to "grow" me. He led me to a tiny
church in Kauai and a "family" who took me to
themselves and loved me—without impeding
God's plan.

Life wasn't always smooth even in that tropical
paradise. When ungratified desires awoke within
me, I was angry that God had left those desires
when He took my husband. What did a person do
with raw and unsatisfied emotions? I questioned
God and His love when I felt miserable and unful-
filled. I wrestled with my emotions as Jacob wrestled with the angel. And then came the still, small
voice. God wanted a complete woman, totally
committed to Him. I understood then that He
wanted every area of my life to be under His will,
with my trust in Him.

After my Jacobean struggle I felt empty but
tranquil. I sat on the bluff, marveling at the symphony of the spindrifting sea crashing against
rocky cliffs, and the loneliness in me cried out to
God for someone by my side to share this wondrous sight. Once again, the still small voice entered my emptiness, *Oh My child, You are sharing it
with Me, the One who created it.*

What joy inexpressible! All was mine to enjoy
with my Lord, my Friend, my Companion.

With my body now finally healed and healthy,
I began to swim and play tennis. I found myself
running one, two, three miles; finally running in
(and finishing!) a 10K run. Like a stream that
winds its way around obstacles, so my emotions

found new outlets in creativity. Great music and literature broadened my mind while God's Word burned itself into my heart. God had not narrowed my scope by removing my desires; He had expanded my horizons as I surrendered what I could not control and explored physical, intellectual, creative and spiritual frontiers.

Opportunity to travel came through newfound friends. I found myself bound for Switzerland with 400 Japanese people as my traveling companions. It was my first experience of leaving America, and I prayed, *Lord, I hope You know where I am.*

At the Swiss chalet, God opened His world before me and honed my senses with sights, sounds and smells and with the taste and touch of His creation. I met people whose friendship has become more precious with the years.

Wherever God directed me to go, I was challenged spiritually. I had lessons to learn, rough edges to be chipped and polished, rebellions and relationships to relinquish to His gentle abrasion. Each step was a trail that led upward out of myself and my grief toward the great call of God. The climb was not easy; the trail was sometimes rocky, but God faithfully led me through the difficult places. He kept me from falling, and the joy of the Lord became my strength.

Years before the death of my husband, God had instructed me to "give thanks in all circumstances" (1 Thessalonians 5:18). I didn't understand the full meaning then, but in obedience, giving thanks became a principle for my life. My attitude changed from negative thoughts and complaining to one of positive thoughts and praise.

Even at the site of the crash, in the blackness above my head, I had seen written the words, "Give thanks in all circumstances." Even then I knew God was there. Whatever happened, He was aware of everything and He was in control. The joy of His presence sustained me through the loneliness and grief that often engulfed me.

Content with God in my singleness, I had committed all future relationships to Him. I asked God if He had another husband for me to please bring him to my doorstep. I couldn't know that He was preparing the heart of Jack Minatra, a widower, as he read an article I had written at the time of my spiritual struggles in Hawaii.

After Jack read the article, he wrote to me and our courtship developed through letters and telephone calls. One day, just before my birthday, I arrived home from work to find Jack Minatra on my doorstep. Two days later, he asked me to marry him. After eleven years of singleness, God gave me another of His wondrous gifts—marriage to Jack. Altogether between us we have seven children and eighteen grandchildren!

God has given us the ministry of hospitality in our Arizona ranch home—where those who visit can find rest and comfort. He has also given us the ministry of marriage whereby we might encourage others.

God has indeed made known to me the path of life and given me the fullness of joy.

*You have made known to me the path of life; you
will fill me with joy in your presence, with eternal pleasures at your right hand. (Psalm 16:11)*

JOYCE ALTHENS MINATRA is a speaker
for retreats, churches and Christian
women's groups. She is author of the
book *When Parents Grow Old,* which is
based on her experience of caring for her
aging parents. She is currently working
on another book, tentatively titled *God
Gave Me Rainbows,* from which the preceding story is excerpted. Joyce is a staff
member with Florence Littauer's Christian Leaders,
Authors and Speakers Seminars (CLASS), Inc. When they
are not traveling, Joyce and her husband Jack can be found
at their ranchette in Florence, Arizona.

CHAPTER 5

BOUNCE BACK FROM FAILURE

*I*f you have experienced failure in school, in your work or in your personal life, you know the heavy, hopeless feeling of defeat. This chapter contains personal stories of how God's promises helped the authors to endure the bleakness of failure—whether long term or only momentary—and bounce back to joyful, fruitful lives.

My flesh and my heart may fail, but God is the strength of my heart and my portion forever. (Psalm 73:26)

Claim Your Blessings

Vincent Muli Kituku

I t was in April 1967 that I experienced the first of many traumatic failures. I was in second grade and it was the school's closing day. Each grade sang, recited a poem or presented a short play to the rest of the school. After my grade's first song, a fellow student, Matthew Wambua, came to me with a message from our teacher: "Muli, Mr. Mwanza told me to tell you not to stand and sing with the others when we sing the next song."

As the class sang the next song, I remained seated. A student from another grade poked me and inquired why I was not singing with the rest. I replied, "I was told not to."

Painful. *I must have sung like a frog*, I thought to myself. The pain of failure registered.

Three years later, in 1970, I tried out for the school choir. Choir members got free uniforms, sang for the president of the country, would be visiting many areas and would be enjoying meals not available for the common man. It was something I eagerly anticipated.

But it was not to be. The choir members stood in four lines to practice. The choir master, Mr. Kiiti, went down the line, listening to the singing of each individual student. When he arrived where I was, he hit my neck with the back side of his hand. That meant I was disqualified to sing in the choir. As I left the group, another choir member said, "Muli, you are tuneless."

It's been over a quarter of a century since that happened, but I still feel a lump in my throat when I remember.

These incidents just confirmed what I had "known," or was made to know, all along—that I was a failure.

Actually, in 1967 I was in the second grade for the second time. I had started first grade in 1963 and progressed through second grade in 1964 and third grade in 1965. Toward the end of the third grade, my father came to the school. He visited with the principal for awhile before I was called in. Students went to the principal's office for only one reason: to be punished. I began to tremble and cry.

The principal said, "Don't worry, Muli, everything will be ok, but you won't be going on to the fourth grade next year. Instead, you will start all over in the first grade." My father nodded and my fate was sealed. There was no explanation. When a student was to repeat a class, he or she had to redo the class for a year. In my case, I was to redo three years.

As it turned out, I didn't go through first grade again. Between 1965 and 1966, my left leg swelled so badly that I couldn't walk. This prevented me from going to school in 1966. By the end of that year, I was well and my parents thought that, because of my body size, that it was appropriate I join the second grade, which I did.

Except for the experience with the school choir, I enjoyed schooling until January 1972, in the seventh grade, when a teacher came to class and ordered me to pick up my stuff and go join the *sixth* grade. What a nightmare! I couldn't understand it. My academic performance had been above average and I ranked between tenth and fifteenth position in a class of sixty students. But once again, I knew the bitter taste of failure.

I completed the sixth grade again, then seventh, then took the high school entrance exam. I failed as expected. I had to remain in primary school, in seventh grade, for another year and then retake the high school entrance exam. I had no other option.

My brother, three years younger than I, was in the same class. To make matters worse, he was an "academic sharpshooter." He ranked first or second in a class of 120. We both were among the best in the class. But no matter how well I did, nobody cared. My brother got the attention. After all, I was a repeater.

However, I went on to high school and later the

University of Nairobi, a very rare occurrence—
less than ten percent of all students countrywide
make it that far.

It was there the Lord saved my soul and I found
that in all the times I failed, He had been there to
keep me going and uplift my spirit. I didn't know
Him at those times, but He knew me before I was
born (see Jeremiah 1:5).

The peace of mind I experienced was more than
I could ask for. I learned that I was created in the
image of the Creator of everything. With that confidence, I went on to graduate from the University
of Nairobi with honors. I received a scholarship to
go to the U.S.A. for further studies at the University of Wyoming, where I began my master's program in range management in 1986.

Then somehow, something went wrong. I had a
family to raise on a $700 per month living allow-
ance. The cultural shock, the different schooling
system and the Wyoming weather all interacted to
make my master's program a most miserable experience. My academic performance was pathetic—I
was told so by some of the professors, but they
didn't have to tell me. I knew. Yet I wanted to ob-
tain a Ph.D.

Some professors were so opposed that the faculty committee had to take a vote. Here is the
tabulation of the vote for Kituku as a Ph.D. candi-
date: four yes, three no, one maybe and one said
nothing. The committee chairman proposed accepting me on a tightly-conditioned, provisional
basis.

One of the professors who voted no had wanted to be my program advisor ever since I came from Africa. I declined his offer because his lifestyle was not compatible with my faith and cultural up-bringing—where adults lead by example. One objection I had to this professor was that he often cursed in the presence of youth.

All this brought back my memories of failure. This time it was more painful than ever, in a foreign land, in the presence of my wife and child. *God, why let this happen?* I didn't want to have anything to do with the professors who voted against my candidacy. I had no idea of what I should do with my life. Go back to Africa as a failure?

In August 1988, in deep despair, I went to a Christian camp meeting. While there, I heard, "Call to me and I will answer you and tell you great and unsearchable things you do not know" (Jeremiah 33:3). I prayed and cast all my cares upon the Lord. Then I heard, " 'For I know the plans I have for you,' declares the LORD, 'plans to prosper you and not to harm you, plans to give you hope and a future' " (Jeremiah 29:11). I left that place with my peace restored, and I determined to do my best under the provisional status.

Two years later, I won first place in the national competition for range management graduate student research papers. My performance at the Ph.D. qualifying exam was beyond the department's expectations. The statistics department offered me a teaching assistant position. In the end, my Ph.D. work was classified as "above average."

In 1993, the professor who had been my "stumbling block" introduced me at an international conference and stated, "Dr. Kituku was one of the best students we have had in our college."

I have learned that others may delay your blessings, but only God can stop blessings from coming your way, unless, of course, you refuse to receive them. Even my early failures in singing have been turned around by God. I have sung solos and with groups and have performances recorded on tape. With God all things are possible to one who believes, takes failure experiences as lessons and refuses to let others determine his or her fate. Failure is not the end if you have hope.

We can rejoice too when we run into problems and trials, for we know that they are good for us—they help us learn to be patient. And patience develops strength of character in us; the more we use it, the more it helps us trust God, until finally our hope and faith are strong and steady. Then we are able to hold our heads high no matter what happens. We know that all is well, for we know how dearly God loves us. Through God's gift of the Holy Spirit we feel this warm love within us, filling our hearts (Romans 5:3-5).

VINCENT MULI KITUKU, Ph.D., the author of *The Voice of Mukamba: African Motivational Folktales for All Ages,* has traveled widely and given seminars, workshops and keynote speeches in Africa, Europe and in several North American states. Dr. Kituku is recognized as a storyteller dedicated to nurturing the human spirit as he speaks on various social aspects of life. He is a graduate of the University of Nairobi, completed his education at the University of Wyoming and now lives with his wife and family in Boise, Idaho.

Burritos with Grace

Neva B. True

*I*f burritos and grace seem an odd combination to you, read on. Until I got better acquainted with them, I cringed at "such irreverence." For me, burritos were for fast-food folks and not on my menu for eating. Grace was for preachers to proclaim and not on my menu for living. Grace was a sacred word meaning "God's unmerited favor." By God's grace I had been saved through faith in Jesus Christ; but that was all past tense. Now the word merely sat on a lofty theological shelf in my heart, not on my menu for each day.

My thinking radically changed about both burritos and grace after the gift of our third child, a beautiful baby boy who arrived when I was forty-three. By the time he started school, my older son was heading off to college, and I had become a great burrito fan. Burritos were quick and easy—just what I needed since my life had moved into the fast lane.

At that time, my aging parents came to live with us. Daddy died the same week our daughter graduated from high school and we encouraged Mother to stay on with us. She did, and God blessed our fifteen years together.

But in times of pressure, my work and my frustrations piled up. I hated to acknowledge stress or tension, as those things did not fit my idea of being a good Christian. I believed being a child of a supernatural God automatically made you Super Mom, flying high above all life's circumstances. But sometimes my wings, trying hard to perform, got so weary they couldn't even flap.

At such times, I would close myself in the bathroom and cry my eyes red. There, with the fan drowning out my words, I would blurt out: "Lord, what am I doing wrong? Why can't I handle everything (and everyone)? I try to make everybody happy, but I'm such a failure at it. Please help me, Lord."

I had turned into a bathroom saint. I even had a Bible there to console, correct, train, instruct and equip me. In that private place, I did a lot of talking to God, updating Him on all that was happening to me. He graciously listened and patiently waited for me to listen to Him.

When failures stack up in your life, do you feel like one big failure? This mind-set trapped me for years. I believed that if I failed, I would be a *complete* failure and people wouldn't look up to me as a godly woman. It was a heavy load I had put upon myself—all the heavier because I thought I had to bear it alone.

The Lord kindly gave me glimpses of truth—like when I blew it and our little boy piped up, "It's ok, Mommie, I knew all along you were no lollipop." I laughed and hugged him, but didn't catch God's love message to me.

During those hurting years I didn't know how to respond rightly to God's invitation to grow in grace and in the knowledge of our Lord Jesus Christ. I could have lived in an atmosphere of grace if I had only been honest with God, myself and others. I could have been growing in the freedom of transparency instead of wilting in the prison of perfectionism.

Emmanuel (God with us) kept showing me His unfailing love regardless of how many times I failed. Emmanuel waits to deliver grace. He will meet us anywhere—even in the bathroom. No appointment needed. No recorded voice. We can pour out everything to Him. He loves us unconditionally.

God's grace and truth were revealed to me one horrendous day. It all started with a flat tire on the "family taxi" which ran regularly (driven by me) back and forth to our son's school, took my beloved mother-in-law to doctor appointments, delivered my ninety-five-year-old mother back and forth to her "Forever Young" club and got me around to deal with all the needs and errands of the family.

On that particular day, the schedule was full. Between errands, I stuck clothes in the washer, discovering later the washer had flooded the service porch, kitchen and family room. The fire department sent the rescue crew to bail me out.

By that evening, the thought of preparing a meal made me groan. I peered hopefully inside the refrigerator for some clue as to what we might be having for dinner. I panicked—it looked like Mother Hubbard's cupboard. "Oh, no! I should have gone shopping," I moaned. Suddenly I spied a package of tortillas behind the milk carton. "Aha," I cried aloud. "Now if I can only find some filling."

As I continued to search frantically, I discovered some slightly wilted veggies and remembered a can of beans. Hope revived. "This will be quick and easy," I encouraged myself. Forcing a smile, I declared, "I'll make this a fun-time meal, in spite of everything."

Soon the yummy filling was ready to be put into the warm tortillas. "Time to eat everyone—a burrito special," I announced cheerfully.

After a moment of thanks, our teenager grabbed for the tortillas. A second later I heard, "Mom, these are moldy!" I stared in disbelief. What else could happen today to make me feel like a total failure?

Remembering that I was supposed to be Super Mom, I rallied to the challenge. "No problem," I reassured the family. "I'll dash to the store and be right back—great burritos coming up!"

The grocery store was just around the corner—God's gracious provision for someone who needs quick help. He can even accelerate the checkout line. His steadfast love was mindful of me that evening as I snatched tortillas, paid in a hurry and rushed out of the store.

All at once I felt the energy drain from my body. I crawled into the car and waves of exhaustion swept over me as I buried my head on the steering wheel. Condemning messages replayed in my mind: *Why don't you give up and quit? You can't do anything right. You'll never learn to plan ahead. Any dummy would have known to check supplies. You are so stupid. You'll always be a failure.*

I pushed back my damp hair and whispered, "Lord, Jesus, I need Your help." Instantly, the faithful Holy Spirit reminded me of an invitation from the Lord Himself: "Come to me, all you who are weary and burdened, and I will give you rest. Take my yoke upon you and learn from me, for I am gentle and humble in heart, and you will find rest for your souls. For my yoke is easy and my burden is light" (Matthew 11:28-30).

I sensed His presence. "Thank You, Lord. I'm coming to You. I want to be yoked to You." I breathed a sigh of release and relief. And then came to mind a verse from Hebrews that seemed a special delivery message straight from God's heart to mine: "Let us then approach the throne of grace with confidence, so that we may receive mercy and find grace to help us in our time of need" (Hebrews 4:16).

With childlike delight I exclaimed, "Lord, that's it! I see it now. Your grace is for times just like I went through today! Right now, I choose to draw near and receive Your mercy and find Your grace for tonight. I thank You for opening my blinded eyes."

My shoulders straightened as I sat tall and confident in the Lord. I realized this was a turning point in my life. No longer would grace sit on a lofty shelf in my heart. Grace, God's grace, would see me through all the "whatevers" of my life. I firmly gripped the steering wheel, stepped on the gas and headed home—singing.

Smiling from my heart, I hurried into the house to serve fresh, hot burritos, with grace.

 NEVA B. TRUE is a published author of articles for a Christian magazine and has written a devotional book. Her various Christian ministries have included youth work, music, discipling women, speaking and writing. She is a graduate of Wheaton College in Christian Education, is married to a pastor and has been blessed with three children and six grandchildren. Neva is now actively retired in Grants Pass, Oregon, where she says the deer are her constant reminders to keep on thirsting for God (see Psalm 42:1-2).

CHAPTER 6

BOUNCE BACK FROM THE PITS

No matter how bad our circumstances, they could be worse. It's a matter of perspective. The quickest way out of "the pits" of self-pity and depression is to adopt an "attitude of gratitude" for the blessings we do have rather than bemoan the absence of those we don't have and believe we should have. The stories in this chapter show how the writers took the words "praise the Lord" to be a command for their daily lives, and how that changed *everything*.

> *The earth beneath barred me in forever. But you brought my life up from the pit, O LORD my God. (Jonah 2:6)*

Special Delivery

Liz Curtis Higgs

*The LORD is my rock, my fortress and my deliv-
erer; my God is my rock, in whom I take refuge.*
(2 Samuel 22:2-3)

The truth is, I didn't always trust in
God. Despite my parents' best efforts
to raise a wholesome, small-town girl,
I veered off track in my mid-teens and started
hanging out with a faster crowd.

First it was sneaking a cigarette out of Mom's
purse. Then it was cutting school for an hour,
then an afternoon, then a whole day. I smoked my
first joint on our senior class trip. Most of the kids
took the bus to New York City—I "flew." A dec-
ade-long love affair with pot began, ironically, on
the steps of the Statue of Liberty.

By my twentieth birthday, I was spending four
and five nights a week on a bar stool, Southern
Comfort in my glass and longing in my eyes. I

found companionship in many but comfort in none.

As a radio personality, I traveled "town to town, up and down the dial" through my twenties, including a stint at a hard rock station in Detroit, where shock-jock Howard Stern did mornings and I did the afternoon show. As a one-sentence summary of how low my values had plummeted, even Howard once shook his head and said, "Liz, you've got to clean up your act!"

By the fall of 1981, I found myself in Louisville, Kentucky, playing oldies at an AM station and playing dangerous games with marijuana, speed, cocaine, alcohol and a promiscuous lifestyle. I'm one of those people who had to go all the way to the bottom of the pit before I was forced to look up for help.

Leaning over my "pit of anger and despair," and extending a hand of friendship, was a husband-and-wife team who had just arrived in town to do the morning show at my radio station. Little did I know that the Lord would use these dear people as my "delivery service."

Although they had enjoyed much worldly success, what these two liked to talk about most was the Lord Jesus Christ. Even more amazing, they seemed to like and accept me "as is." (Can you imagine what they must have thought when we met? *Now, here's a project!*)

But they didn't treat me like a project, a package that needed to be delivered from sin to salvation. They treated me like a friend who needed to know that being delivered was an option. Simply put, they loved me with a love so compelling that I was powerless to resist it.

I remember February 21, 1982, like it was yesterday. It was my seventh Sunday to visit my friends' church, and by then I was singing in the choir. When we closed the service singing, "I Have Decided to Follow Jesus," I did just that. I walked right out of the choir loft and down to the baptistry, as the whole alto section gasped: "We thought she was one of us!" Finally, I was.

I was delivered from one location to another, from the gates of hell to the gates of heaven—"absolutely, positively overnight!"

Lord, may I never forget the price You paid for my delivery.

From *Reflecting His Image: Discovering Your Worth in Christ from A to Z* by Liz Curtis Higgs ©1996 Thomas Nelson Publishers. Used by permission.

 After a decade as a popular radio personality in five states, LIZ CURTIS HIGGS moved onto the stage as a conference and retreat speaker for businesses, hospitals, associations and churches. Her fourth and most recent book, *Reflecting His Image*, was published in 1996 and her first children's book, *The Pumpkin Patch Parable*, was published in the fall of 1995. Liz is a member of National Speakers Association and has the prestigious designations CSP (Certified Speaking Professional) and CPAE (Council of Peers Award for Excellence) awarded by that organization. She resides in Louisville, Kentucky.

A Cross of Dental Gold

Naomi Rhode

He was a good-looking Texas dentist, with his white starched shirt open at the neck, exposing a beautiful gold cross.

We were having a coffee break at our seminar. As a speaker I am passionate about presenting material as excellently as I can because I hope to be a facilitator of life changes. This often occurs one-on-one, which makes the breaks as important as the sessions.

He stood alone in apparent contemplation. Observing others? Lost in his own thoughts and plans? Troubled? Leery?

I approached him prayerfully. (I like the peace and courage of that style of communication.)

"Good morning. That's a beautiful cross you are wearing—would you tell me about it?" I asked.

He smiled slightly and said he "wasn't ready to." The strange reply signaled that here was a

special story, possibly even a life-changing saga. I
wondered if I would ever be privileged to hear the
story.

If seminars work the way they should, they become islands of exploration, of learning, of changing
and of growth. Strangers coming together from different parts of the country provide fertile ground to
be tilled and planted. Although they may share a
common profession, they have vastly differing personal problems and perspectives. The safety of ano-
nymity stimulates a kind of open communication
and sharing that doesn't usually happen in home
territory.

Saturday arrived. It was the last day of the
seminar. Bonds had been established. The communication, both personal and professional, had
been richly rewarding. It was the last coffee break.
Isn't peripheral vision amazing? You know when
someone is approaching, and sometimes you even
know *why*.

"I'm ready to tell you about the cross," the
Texan said, smiling.

He told the following story with directness and
candor. He said:

I have always made a point of doing whatever I do with great fervor and passion.
Most of the time that made me very successful. Dental school was that way for me. My
practice was that way, my marriage and
family were all that way. I had it made. Life
was going great for me.

Then, like a lot of foolish young men, I got involved in drugs and alcohol. But remember, I was the type that doesn't *dabble* in anything. As usual, I went all the way. "High risk equals the greatest reward" was my philosophy. And with that attitude, it didn't take long to hit bottom. I got so heavily addicted I finally lost everything that mattered: my first marriage, my family, and I even came close to losing my dental practice. I had bought $20,000 worth of drugs and now meandered through my days, looking forward to the abyss of each weekend—when I could block out the horror and the truth of my wrecked reality.

On one certain Friday, my anticipation for the numbness of the weekend was high, but my plans were thwarted by my cousin's incessant invitation that I attend an evening service with him at his church. I resisted. He persisted. I was irritated, I was angry, but I finally gave in. I don't know why I went. Perhaps it was only because of his stubborn persistence. Perhaps it was a flash of curiosity—a desire to peek into the source of another person's peace. Or maybe I just wanted another opportunity to ridicule, as I had in the past, what I called the "ridiculous religiosity" of my "naive" and "misguided" relative.

But I went. I told myself it was ludicrous—but I went.

Behind a barely polite facade, I laughed inside myself at the worshipers and at their simple service of worship.

I went home that night and sank into my drug-infested cocoon of depression and despair. Saturday morning brought more self-hatred and the same oblivion from reality.

About 3 o'clock that afternoon, while I thought I was securely hidden from the world, suddenly and inexplicably, *He* found me. Yes, it's true. Jesus came into my room. I saw Him. It doesn't matter what people say—He came. Jesus Christ was visible to me in all His glory. His radiance blinded me. His power overwhelmed me. His truth humbled me. I fell on my knees—all my regrets, my sins and my stupidity I laid at His feet. He forgave me, and in an instant He changed me. I was hidden away in a drug stupor; still He found me and for some unknown reason reached out to me—and I responded. I rejoiced, knowing my life would never be the same again.

The next day I went early to my dental office.

With a new fervor, a new passion and the promise of a newly redeemed excellence, I felt I needed a physical symbol of that transformation. I thought about Christ's sacrifice on the cross to save my wretched soul. I took some dental gold and carefully fashioned it into this cross. It would be the symbol of my transformation. I put it on a gold chain and have not taken it off since that day.

God has richly blessed me since the day I repented and gave my life to Him. I have a lovely new wife, a new family, an incredible dental practice and a bright new future and hope.

As he ended his story of personal struggle and pain—and now new purpose and joy—he reached back and released the clasp of his chain. I stood in total disbelief as he placed the beautiful gold cross necklace around my neck and said, "Naomi, because you truly love people—because you care so deeply that they come to the cross—I want you to have this."

That cross of dental gold is a symbol of one person's spiritual transformation. For me, it is also a precious gift that helps me remember to ask people, "Will you tell me about your cross?"

 NAOMI RHODE, RDH (Registered Dental Hygenist), CSP (Certified Speaking Professional), CPAE (Council of Peers Award for Excellence), is past president of the National Speakers Association and is known for her inspirational speaking, both to general and health care audiences. She is co-owner and vice-president of SmartPractice, a marketing and manufacturing company which provides products and services to the health care industry. Naomi is the author of two inspirational gift books,

The Gift of Family—A Legacy of Love and *More Beautiful Than Diamonds—The Gift of Friendship.* Naomi and her husband live in Phoenix, Arizona.

CHAPTER 7

BOUNCE BACK FROM BROKEN DREAMS

roken dreams—our own or those of our loved ones—test our faith and can destroy our belief in the future. The Spirit of God can broaden our horizons and inspire us to action when we dare to catch the vision of what God wants for us—not just what we want. The stories in this chapter tell of broken dreams that resulted in greater faith as each of the writers, in their own time and in their own way, reflected on God's sovereignty and His loving purpose for us.

He heals the brokenhearted and binds up their wounds. (Psalm 147:3)

Clean Sweep

Patsy Clairmont

Feeling zonked, I decided to zone out when I boarded the plane bound for home. I found my row and secretly checked out my seat companion. She was a normal, fiftyish-looking woman. (I immediately liked her for being older than I was.) I peeked at her so I wouldn't be obligated conversationally. I didn't want anything to disrupt my siesta in the sky.

Doesn't it just drive you bonkers when you have a hidden agenda and someone toddles into your space and trips up your plan?

This time my "toddler" was a flight attendant who came scooting down the aisle offering treats. My stomach won out over sleep, and I ended up chatting with my neighbor, Susan. Am I glad I did! This was no normal woman.

Susan told me an incredibly sad story with a surprise ending. She said her beloved husband of

thirty years decided he loved someone else and
wanted a divorce. The feelings of crushing be-
trayal deepened when Susan found out his affair
had been going on for years. He was also a clever
businessman and had prepared himself for this decision so that he would come out the financial
winner.

Susan was first numb and then paralyzed by
her grief. Her husband used her shock to his ad-
vantage, swooping down fast and furious to get all
he could. Much to Susan's dismay, she was noti-
fied by the court that she would have to turn over
to her husband and his girlfriend her cherished
home of twenty-three years where they had raised
their five children.

Reeling from grief upon grief, Susan moved
into a tiny, furnished apartment. There she tried
to figure out what had gone wrong. In the divorce
settlement, she was awarded a small, failing business that was to be her source of income. To add
not only to her dilemma but also to her pain, her
ex-husband and his female friend opened a new,
competing business just down the street.

Now, folks, I don't know about you, but that's
where I would throw up my hands and spit.

Not Susan. She reached inside and pulled up
her faith. She decided she couldn't allow others'
choices to extinguish her joy or decree her future.
She was determined not to be a victim but to be
victorious and begin with a grateful heart. No, she
wasn't grateful for her tremendous loss but that
God is the Healer of fractured hearts.

One day while doing dishes, Susan turned on the small TV near her sink. As she changed channels, she came to a musical presentation and was caught up in the contagious melody. But now she had no dance partner.

Then she spotted her companion leaning against the cupboard. He was the tall, silent type. She waltzed over and embraced the kitchen broom, then twirled about the room, laughing and singing. Around and around she spun, dizzy with delight. Suddenly she realized she was not alone.

Susan saw she had been joined by three of her married daughters who were standing in the doorway, giggling at their mother's antics. (They checked on her regularly those days for fear her losses would be more than she could bear, driving her to an act of despair.)

As she stood holding her silent partner, Susan looked at her girls and said, "In the years to come, may this be the way you remember me . . . dancing."

Susan didn't want to leave a legacy of brokenness or despair. Instead, she chose to give a living heritage of courage, conviction and yes, celebration. Her circumstances were anything but normal, but then, so was her response.

By the way, she was able to turn the little business around, buy a lovely home and enjoy a full and active life. She chose not to stay in her sorrow or linger in her loss, but in the midst of devastation, to dance.

Patsy Clairmont is the author of several bestselling books that combine a fast-paced humor with her knowledge of God's Word and an understanding of human nature. Her latest book, *Sportin' a 'Tude*, provides witty and scriptural suggestions for keeping one's attitude in balance. Patsy lives in Brighton, Michigan, with her husband and two sons. She speaks throughout the United States, providing humor and hope for Christian retreats, luncheons, seminars and workshops.

Fear of Success

Nancy Moser

I had big plans—but God had bigger plans.

One of my favorite pastimes used to be musing over the grand future of my writing career. Every phone call brought hope. The mailman was my dearest friend—or worst enemy. Each day the sound of his mail truck revived a new clenching in my stomach. *Was today the day my dreams would come true?*

My plans involved getting a New York agent who would sell my mystery novel to a New York publisher. My advance had a long string of zeros. The book would be a huge success. I would travel the nation on a book tour and become buddies with Oprah.

I knew what I was going to wear, what I was going to say and how I was going to break the marvelous news to my family. I nursed these daydreams for a year. Then suddenly, obtrusively, a new dimension was added to my thoughts of book tours and fame. . . . *Fame would rip me away from my family for weeks at a time. My children would forget my face. I'd miss their band concerts and baseball games. My husband Mark would discover a better way to fix leftover hamburger and figure out how to fold towels so they'd fit in the linen closet without the door bulging open. The house plants would thrive in my absence.*

I tried to push away these traitorous thoughts. Why were my lovely dreams being tainted by this fear—this fear of success?

I'd heard the rousing pep talks of speakers who said I was sabotaging myself by letting negative thoughts enter my consciousness. Talking in the exclamation points and capital letters that are their mainstay, they admonished me: Think POSITIVE! Want it! Work for it! The world is YOURS!

"But . . . ," I'd say.

"No buts!" they'd say.

"But my family . . . ," I'd say.

They had no answers. So I continued to be afraid, my excitement drowning in a sea of fear. *My way isn't working, Lord. Take away this fear. Show me how to have success Your way.*

Little did I know I was about to be both humbled *and* lifted up with a single blow.

This emotional roller coaster started with a rejection—which, considering I'm a writer, was nothing new. Unfortunately, it was also something I never got used to. The New York publishing world took great delight in dashing my dreams. They made me feel privileged if my work was read at all. So, having found an agent who had actually agreed to read my entire mystery manuscript, I had high hopes—until I opened the mailbox and saw a large padded envelope.

My manuscript. Back from the New York agent. My heart fell to my toes as my big plans were crushed.

I hurried to the house so I could be miserable in private. I took the manuscript into the bedroom and shut the door. I opened the envelope and pulled out the letter. A personalized rejection. At least it wasn't a form letter.

As I read the letter, I wished for the polite aloofness of a form letter. Not only did this agent not want to represent my book, she found the humorous style of the main character "tiresome." And considering my novel was written entirely from that character's viewpoint, her letter translated: She didn't like my style.

Not liking the fact there was a dead body under the bed or that the story took place in a town with a population of 1,534 would have been a slap on my wrist. But not liking my style—the way I wrote—was a slap in my face. And it stung.

Do You want me to quit, Lord? I thought my writing was a gift, but maybe it's all in my head. . . .

I knew I wasn't alone in my insecurities. Everyone faces rejection—no matter what his or her calling. Careers roadblocked, dreams sidetracked. At some point the choice has to be made to give up or . . .

My mind reeled at such thoughts. I was meant to write. I knew it. I just had to find the right path.

I marched to my computer, determined to "fix" my book to fit the taste of this New York agent. Chapter 1 filled the screen. *Serious. Make the main character serious.* Forget that the character would like to drown in a plate of sausage-gravy biscuits, forget she liked men with dimples, forget her not-quite-spotless driving record, forget the fact she wished she were two inches shorter. Forget—

—to follow the advice of this New York agent?

I stopped typing, stopped trying to force my main character into a foreign mold.

The agent was wrong.

My style was right, at least for me. Although I hadn't had any luck getting my novel published as yet, I *was* getting a lot of inspirational humor accepted—articles that were written in the same style as when I wrote about my hapless heroine.

But what about the wisdom of this hotshot New York agent? I was just an underconfident Midwestern writer. Who was I to say she was wrong?

Instead of conjuring up my dream of success, I set it aside. I bowed my head. *I'm tired of worrying, Lord. You gave me this talent. It's Yours. Show me what to do with it. Show me how to please You.*

The next morning when I tried to write I experienced an odd sensation. It was like my thoughts were bumper cars, bouncing, swirling, but never getting anywhere. After an hour of trying to make my ideas behave, I turned my computer off.

I sat in front of the blank screen. *What's going on, Lord?*

God chose to remain silent.

Having free time before me, I set off to do errands. Library books returned, kitty litter bought, banking done. I found myself near my favorite Christian bookstore. I pulled in. I bypassed the music and nonfiction sections—my usual pit stops—and took a detour down the fiction aisle.

"May I help you?" asked a friendly clerk.

A question popped into my head. "Is there such a thing as a Christian mystery?"

"Certainly," she said, moving to a shelf. "And there are thrillers, science fiction, romances and westerns. Almost every genre is covered by Christian publishers these days. It's a growing market."

I picked up a slick paperback—larger than the normal pocket size. Full-color cover. Nice graphics. I read the back. A story about real people, flawed people who had not-so-perfect driving records, who ate the wrong foods and were unsure of themselves.

My heart began to pound. *Was this it? Was this the answer?*

I grabbed three books, paid and rushed to my car.

I looked at the publishers listed in the books. Forget the imposing publishing world of New York. These publishers hailed from Tennessee,

Michigan, Illinois and Pennsylvania. Hometown
places for hometown people. *Hometown people like
me?*

In a moment of wondrous revelation, everything fell into place, like puzzle pieces tumbling
from heaven. There was no reason to be afraid
anymore.

Since Christian book publishers would realize
how important it was that I be at my daughter's
violin concert and my son's baseball game, surely
they'd be kind and understanding. Surely I could
trust them to treat me fairly. Surely I could de-
velop a relationship with them based on honesty,
integrity and a shared love of God. I could be a
fish in a pond, not a minnow struggling in an
ocean.

I cried tears of release. The mere words,
"Thank you" were inadequate to express the joy
that consumed me. *God is so wise.* The *fear* was a
gift from Him. The *rejection* was a gift from Him.
And now, the *answer* is a gift from Him.

I hurried home to work on my novel. I read the
pages with new purpose. I put back the references
to my heroine's spiritual feelings—the parts I'd
left out to make the story fit the generalities of the
mainstream marketplace. I made her whole. I gave
her back to God.

She still loves sausage gravy on warm biscuits
and she is still attracted to dimpled men. She continues to drive her car too fast and occasionally
she apologizes to God for complaining about her
height. But now she's alive. She's real.

I'm no longer afraid. I don't have to be. Because I have the best Agent in the universe—One who is more than capable of handling every detail of my dreams.

I know God has big plans for me. And by trusting Him, I'm already a success.

NANCY MOSER finds that twenty-one years of marriage, three children and the continued encouragement of an ever-patient God has created a wealth of material for her writing. An inspirational speaker, she is the author of over forty-five inspirational humor articles as well as two books due out in 1997: *Motherhood: Take This Job and Love It* and *Save Me God, I Fell in the Carpool.* Nancy lives in Overland Park, Kansas.

I've Got to Hand It to You

Patty Stump

Anger often creeps in subtly and takes root without warning. Hurts and disappointments can silently compound themselves within our hearts. Then, when we least expect it, our pent-up emotions erupt, often wounding those we love and commonly testing the depth and foundation of our relationship with God.

For me, anger silently took root during a season when a number of long-standing dreams and cherished relationships painfully crumbled. I was in a long-term relationship which I *assumed* was leading to marriage. I was confident the pieces would fall into place and that we would always continue to share common goals and interests, church involvements and our close circle of friends. In making plans for the future, I had come to *assume* my desires would naturally take shape. Why shouldn't they? Surely God wanted these things for me as well! I couldn't imagine my life veering from the path I'd chosen. Yet as time passed so did the hopes and dreams that laced my plans together.

My neatly ordered life now lay in fragmented pieces as the relationship unraveled, impacting not only our lives, but others' lives as well. I was unprepared for the strain that occurred in a handful of mutual friendships and found myself torn between feelings of disbelief, anger and grief. Why had God allowed these things to happen? Didn't He care? He seemed removed and silent. Standing in my bedroom in the wee hours of the morning, feeling alone and abandoned by God, I shook my clenched fist toward heaven and sarcastically exclaimed, "Fine. You take my life and see what You can do!"

Looking back, I realize a sobering truth; I'd never really given my desires, my plans or my life up to God. I had not relied upon Him. I had looked to Him for His blessing, *not His will*. I had never taken into consideration *His* desires for my life. In the midst of my disappointing circumstances, I certainly did not believe He could "work all things together for good" (see Romans 8:28). My disbelief had given root to bitterness, and my heart was spiritually aloof and distrustful of God.

Now what? As I stood in my room that night, I realized I was at a crossroad. I could either continue my course and salvage what was left amidst the remnants, or I could hand my life over to Him. I had little to lose in giving Him a chance to make sense of my anger and brokenness. If He was true to His Word, these times would work together for His good. Could I believe Him? It seemed as if everyone else had let me down, would He as well?

These are common questions when one is working through anger, disappointment and broken dreams. God desires to walk through those uncertainties with us, enabling us to take the steps through brokenness to wholeness in Christ.

My first step in working through my shaken faith was to decide whether or not I would yield to God my heart, hopes and hurts, believing Him to be true to His Word. This initial step determines whether we will direct our own steps or rely on God. This requires not only believing in God but *yielding* to God as well, accepting Him as both our Savior and the Lord of our lives. Proverbs 3:5-6 states that we must trust in the Lord with *all* of our heart, relying on Him to direct our paths.

Before I could feel that trust again, I had to first return to these basics: *Yes, I do believe God is true to His Word, and yes, I do desire for Him to be both my Savior and Lord*. Next, I recommitted myself to exploring His truths. After all, those truths are for His children, and I was one of His own.

The first truth I wanted to rely upon was His promise to work all things together "for the good of those who love him, who have been called according to his purpose" (Romans 8:28). Loving Him involved both trusting Him and walking in obedience to His standards and will for my life. I decided to take my hands off the reins and give Him a chance.

The second truth I claimed was Jeremiah 29:11: " 'For I know the plans I have for you,' declares the LORD, 'plans to prosper you and not to harm you, plans to give you hope and a future.' " I struggled to believe in the future, although my hope was nonexistent. In order to go any further with Him I had to take Him at His Word and step out in faith. Second Corinthians 5:7 says: "We live by faith, not by sight." I prayed for Him to strengthen my faith and remove my unbelief, still a bit skeptical yet excited about what He might have in store.

As I began to discover God in the midst of the fragments, I realized I had unfinished business to tend to—asking His forgiveness. I knew I needed to ask His forgiveness for the anger and hardness of my heart. I had to let those emotions go before they became a permanent way of life. Next I sought His forgiveness for the various ways I had strayed from His path, taking my life into my own hands. Somewhere along the way I had invited Him to be a part of my life, rather than giving my life to Him. He had never abandoned me. It was I who had turned my back on Him. "If we confess our sins, he is faithful and just and will forgive us our sins and purify us from all unrighteousness" (1 John 1:9).

Over time I began to adjust my priorities. My anger didn't instantly vanish but it did begin to diminish as I consistently placed my trust and dependence in God. I no longer shook my fist at Him, but instead sought to offer up to Him whatever treasure was clenched in my palm. There have been moments when I have wanted to pull away, fearful He would take what I have come to treasure. On other occasions I have been thankful He took what I handed to Him and replaced it with a much grander delight.

Anger, hurt and broken dreams will certainly occur. Is God big enough to see me through the obstacles and challenges of life? Can He really bring wholeness from the broken pieces? Does He have a future and a hope for me? *Indeed!* He is faithful to His Word and His children.

As He weaves my fragments back together, I am both humbled and amazed at how He works with what I have to offer Him. And, in those moments when I catch a glimpse of His divine handiwork, I am thrilled that *finally* I can hand it to Him!

PATTY STUMP, M.Ed., CPC, is a minister's wife, mother of two, Christian marriage and family counselor, freelance writer and frequent speaker for women's events, marriage seminars and weekend retreats. Patty communicates scriptural truths and steps for personal, practical application using humor, wisdom and excitement. She and her family live in Glendale, Arizona.

The Name Amy Means "Beloved"

Barbara Geraghty

*T*he day was memorable, most of all because of the serendipity of the final outcome. I was treating my best friend, Laura, to lunch at a restaurant for her birthday. I had stopped by my mailbox to get my mail as I left for our luncheon date. Among the usual bills, flyers and advertisements, I discovered a letter from my daughter Amy.

I smiled as I recognized the charming stationery I had recently sent her. The return address read:

The Musick Facility

I was running a little late and there wasn't time to read the letter then, so I stuffed it in my purse. *Maybe I'll share Amy's news, whatever it is, with Laura,* I thought to myself. *Laura's always been fond of Amy.*

At the time of my lunch date with Laura, Amy

was just about at the bottom of the pit. She had been through intensive counseling, anti-depressants, drug rehabilitation programs and abusive relationships. She was now twenty-two and in jail in a facility on Musick Street—euphemistically called the Musick Facility.

Laura had moved into my Fullerton home with us several years earlier when she and I were both students at California State University, Fullerton. I was a thirty-two-year-old single mom struggling with a conflict between my desire to provide a stable home for my two daughters and my urge to be free of responsibility. Laura was a twenty-two-year-old with a gift for dodging responsibility, but I had taken her into my home anyway and, over the years, she became the best friend I ever had.

Amy was ten at that time, a lovable child despite being frustrated by learning disabilities. She was the type of child whose report card read: "Lacks motivation; missing and late assignments; a pleasure to have in class."

Later, Laura and I both married and became happily involved and successful in our respective careers. But life had not been kind to my Amy. She started by making poor choices in friends and progressed to drug involvement and eventually running away. And now here she was in jail.

For years I had prayed for this wayward child of mine, but it seemed to me God wasn't listening to my prayers. I thought of Proverbs 22:6: "Train up a child in the way he should go: and when he is old, he will not depart from it" (KJV). I prayed that this would apply to Amy, but my fears for her were overwhelming.

Just one month before my lunch with Laura, with a heavy heart, I had finally given up on Amy. After doing everything I could think of to solve Amy's problems, I quit! I surrendered the life of my beloved child to God.

Laura and I sat there in the restaurant for a long time talking about the latest developments in our respective careers. When it was time for us to leave, I handed Amy's note to Laura to read while I went to pay the check. When I came back, I saw tears in Laura's eyes. She didn't say much but gave me a sympathetic smile through her tears.

Two days later, Laura called me. "I'm only calling to let you know what I'm going to do," she said, "but I don't want you to get involved. God has kept me awake for the last two nights, telling me to invite Amy to come live with my family and take care of our kids for me after she is released from jail. I'm going to do it."

I could hardly believe my ears. Can you imagine any sane mother of three very young, extremely vulnerable children inviting a drug user, someone who is attracted to violent ex-convicts and who has just been released from jail to come live in her home and care for her children while she is away at work?

But she followed through, and Amy went to live in her home. Laura set only one ground rule for Amy. She could not use drugs when she was at

their home. Her weekends off were her own to do
with as she pleased. When Amy talked to Laura
about any issue, Laura would say, "I trust you,
Amy. Use your own judgment."

Within the first week, the kids loved Amy and
Amy loved the kids. She was embraced by a very
special family, a family who did not judge her or
advise her, but simply enjoyed her for who she
was. Within five months, Amy was clean and so-
ber and happy. Seven months later, she enrolled
in college. A few months after that she got a part-
time retail sales job, where, on her first day, she
sold just about everything they had there to sell.

This miraculous change had taken place only
after I totally and completely surrendered Amy to
God. I still remember every word of the prayer I
cried aloud when Amy was put in jail: "Dear Lord
God, I've done all I can do. Now I give her to
You, Lord. If it is Your will that she die of AIDS
or a drug overdose or be beaten to death, so be it. I
trust You. Thy will be done."

If you are struggling to help someone you love
escape the ravages of self-destructive behavior,
perhaps this story will help you. If you are a parent, perhaps you can imagine the fear and heart-
break of even contemplating the awful possibilities
of what could have happened to Amy. Giving her
up to God was, in my whole life, the ultimate test
of my faith. In my whole life, God's giving her
back to me was the ultimate miracle.

BARBARA GERAGHTY is a professional speaker and author. Her special ties include a new paradigm of selling skills, Visionary Selling™ and an interactive sales training game called Klue. She lives in Irvine, California, is president of Idea Quest in Orange County and is a member of National Speakers Association.

CHAPTER 8

BOUNCE BACK FROM PHYSICAL CHALLENGE

*W*e pray for healing when we, or someone we love, is faced with an illness or ongoing physical challenge. It is difficult for us to accept that healing is not always part of God's plan. Many people prayed for the healing of Christopher Reeve after the riding accident that paralyzed him from the neck down. God did not see fit to grant those prayers. Why? We trust that God planned to use this man's infirmity for a higher purpose. Most of us know personally of times when God *has* granted His healing in answer to prayer. The authors in this chapter learned to trust and found that God's decision, in their own case, was the right one.

My comfort in my suffering is this: Your promise preserves my life. (Psalm 119:50)

A Song of Victory

Kathie Clarke

*M*y uncle Bill's family was plunged into fear and uncertainty when he began to lose his memory, repeat himself and retreat into a world of confusion. They didn't want to accept the opinion of the first doctor, so they sought other opinions. The other doctors confirmed the diagnosis of Alzheimer's disease.

Uncle Bill had been a successful engineer, a talented musician and a loving family man. Those around him began to notice him constantly forgetting where things were and what day it was, getting confused if he was anywhere but home and losing his place when he sang in the choir. After making a wrong turn and ending up miles from home, he was no longer allowed to drive. He became fearful when left alone and confused whenever he was in new surroundings.

I watched him at family gatherings. At first he

153

would try to enter conversations, but ended up re-
peating himself over and over. Later, unsure of
what to say, he became more and more silent. My
heart ached for him and for his immediate family.
I knew my aunt was troubled and so was I. I wondered how God keeps His children spiritually
when they have a problem mentally. Only later
did I come to understand.

After my uncle's death, my aunt related the following story about an incident that happened in
the latter days of his illness when he could no
longer remember even familiar things and was in
constant confusion.

Someone from the church had called a few days
before Christmas to say that the choir would be
coming over to sing carols to them that evening. It
was bitterly cold outside and when the doorbell
rang she hurried to let them in. As they crowded
into the warmth of the living room they weren't
sure what to say. They had come to sing to their
old friend, but they seemed unsure of what reaction they would get from him. Uncle Bill stood
quietly at first, seeming not to comprehend what
they they were doing, watching as they turned
their song sheets to the right page.

They began their singing with "Joy to the
World." As they sang the words, ". . . let every
heart prepare Him room," Bill began singing
along with them, *every word perfect*, springing forth
from a reservoir within. Many eyes within the
choir became blurry as they realized that a miracle
was happening, a confirmation that deep within

Bill his soul was still guarded by the One whose birthday they were celebrating in song.

Not long after that, my uncle went to be with his Lord.

After his funeral, I sat down alone to try to find an answer to my questions about the mind and the soul. My concern seemed to resolve itself as I wrote down the thoughts that came to me about God's ultimate victory for my uncle and for all those who are His. I hope this poem from my heart will be a help to those who ponder a similar situation.

The Victor

Not a contest of wills, a test of strength
or battle for power.
What was occurring was a struggle
of life and death
Within the mind of the man bent ever
so slightly by the
Fourscore and five years he had lived
upon the earth.

Within this man was a light that had
been lit many years before.
It shone out through his actions and words.
It lit up his eyes and his smile
And made his corner of the earth a brighter place.

The invisible enemy, whose only purpose
is to destroy,
Began the fight, taking a memory here, a bit of
knowledge there,
Trying to get to the light, but always
falling short because

Light can never be conquered by darkness.
As a lifetime of memories slipped away,
one at a time,
Day after day, the man always knew the light
And who He was who dwelt there.

When a melody of joy was lifted to celebrate the holy birth
Long-forgotten words spilled from his lips
And he joined in the song of praise.
And as the man's days grew dim and
death was near,
Always the light was there, covering his fear
And keeping away the darkness.

Then, when it was time to cross the final barrier,
He who is the Light of the world took
the man's hand
And together they walked to a place
already familiar
Because it was illuminated by the Son of God.

In the end, the man had won victory
over the enemy.
For the enemy can never touch our soul, take away the
light,
Or separate us from the love of God.
In loving memory of my uncle,
William Quentin Kehr,
September 28, 1909-January 4, 1994

Now, in all these things we are more than conquerors through him who loved us. For I am convinced that neither death nor life, neither angels nor demons, neither the present nor the future, nor any powers, neither height nor depth, nor anything else in all creation, will be able to separate

*us from the love of God that is in Christ Jesus our
Lord. (Romans 8:37-39)*

KATHIE CLARKE and her husband are
both teachers at Maranatha Academy, a
Christian school in Shawnee, Kansas.
They live on thirty acres of woods by a
lake with several domestic and a few wild
animals. Kathie enjoys writing about
children and about the experiences she
has had that might be of help to others.
She has five children and seven grandchildren.

Does God Care?

Robert Treash

February 26, 1983. Whenever I hear that date mentioned my heart skips a beat. After all, that was the night my heart stopped beating.

The preceding year had been the happiest of my life. As a senior in high school I led an active athletic and social life. I was president of the youth group at my family's church. I was accepted at three colleges, but had chosen one in New England, just far enough away to be independent but still near enough to be able to come home often.

I was home for a break from college. The youth group I had led invited me to take part in a game night at a local gym. Afterward Tom (not his real name), Dave and I headed to an ice cream parlor. I squeezed into the backseat of Tom's tiny old car. Dave got in the front and we rolled out of the parking lot.

My memory ends there, but I learned later that as we drove down the road, the car swerved, and I called to Tom to stop fooling around. "I can't help it!" he yelled back.

An engine mount had fallen off our car, and we swerved into a lane of oncoming traffic. Tom's small Dodge collided with a Cadillac. Dave, who sat in the path of the collision, died at the scene of the crash.

In the first few hours at St. Vincent's Hospital in Bridgeport, ConneCticut, my prognosis didn't look good—my heart actually stopped beating for a couple of minutes. I was comatose for the next two-and-a-half months.

I drifted in and out of the coma. With no memory of the accident, I remember being terrified of what these people they called "doctors" were doing. I was convinced these "evil people" were up to no good. Perhaps they were performing experiments on me! When anyone entered my room, I would pretend to be asleep. I was devising a plan to escape, and they mustn't suspect anything.

Daily the "wicked people" in white surrounded my bed, lifted my torso and slid an angled vinyl pillow under me so that I lay on my stomach on it. I'd never before felt such searing pain! I couldn't lift myself—my right arm had atrophied and they kept me from using my left.

These devils! I thought. *They're gonna kill me!*

It was a long time before someone explained to me that they were stretching the scar from surgery that ran the length of my belly.

I gradually came out of the coma. But learning to walk and talk again was a long, hard process. I remember the confusion of having in mind exactly what I wanted to say—with the emphasis in the right place, with proper intonation—and not being able to articulate it. I'd open my mouth to speak, but no sound would come out.

I remember being unable to do things I didn't even have to think about before. I recall lying flat on a mat and being told to hold my right arm straight in the air. After trying and failing, I screamed exasperatedly to myself, *I can't even do* that?!

Nowadays I never take walking or talking or even simple arm movements for granted; I often remind myself that these are gifts, not rights.

I know now, though I wasn't aware of it then, that God was with me, watching over me all the way through my ordeal. For example, I remember the collar that was supposed to prevent me from turning my head; I didn't know that my neck was broken, and I kept trying to take it off. The Lord protected me even when I wasn't aware of it; by the time I could move enough to attempt to free myself from the collar, my neck was pretty well healed.

As time went on, I experienced tremendous healing and even went on to graduate from college, which is astounding considering what had happened. But afterward it was no bed of roses. I had difficulty landing and keeping a job. I went through a spiritual dry spell and began to question God.

God's provision during the initial stages of my

recovery had encouraged faith in all those close to my situation. Witnessing everything come to-gether so perfectly left no doubt in their minds that God's hand was in it. They told me stories of His goodness to me, and I was thankful. I believed God had been working for my good.

But now something was missing: God seemed absent, almost like He had let me go. Like the Israel-ites wandering in the wilderness, and particularly the younger generation who learned only second-hand about God's deliverance of the Israelites from the bondage of Egypt, I too began to question His provision. *If God really cares,* I reasoned, *why doesn't He show me* now, *while I am conscious?"*

Aha! That's what was missing! It occurred to me that all of my "miracles" had happened while I was unconscious. I believed others when they told me what God had done, but it was all secondhand. In retrospect, I realize now that probably the best (nonspiritual) gift God has ever given me was the coma; because of it I missed a lot of pain, and He worked wonders for me physically "while I was sleeping." But at the bottom of my pit of despair about ten years after the accident, fearing that God had abandoned me, I wanted (challenged?) God to give me a sign—something I could experience con-sciously; some evidence that He was still there and cared for me—now, not just then!

It was a brazen demand, perhaps, but it came from the bottom of my heart with urgency. And God must have heard it as a sincere prayer, for He was not long in granting it!

At the time I was regularly attending a friend's Bible study. One night two visitors were there— Ed Voccola and his fiancée, Lynn. I introduced myself: "Hello, I'm Bob. I don't believe we've met."

Ed looked at me with a sly grin. "Oh, I think we have."

"Really? I'm sorry, I don't remember. . . ."

"I'm not surprised. You were hardly in a condition to remember anything."

Now I've never been drunk, and my memory's usually pretty good. The only time I wouldn't have been able to remember—the only time he could be referring to—was the accident!

"Were you . . . there?" I asked, my voice beginning to quiver.

Ed affirmed that yes, he was there, and he told me the following story:

He was off duty the night of February 26 and eating at a restaurant across from the ice cream parlor that was our destination the night of the crash. When he finished eating, he got in his car and drove—right into the accident scene. Tom had just emerged from the car, grasping his injured hand, pleading for someone to help his friends.

Ed was an emergency medical technician. He called for support, then ran to our car. He looked in the front seat and realized there was nothing he could do to save Dave. So he turned his attention to me.

I was sitting upright with eyes wide open, gasp-

ing for air. My right side was caved in, my lung
collapsed. The part of the brain that controls
breathing was damaged. Ed had to get oxygen to
me fast.

He climbed into the back seat and administered
mouth-to-mouth resuscitation, being careful not
to move my neck. He "breathed" for me for thirty
minutes while other emergency personnel worked
to get me out using the jaws of life. If the fracture
had worsened or if my broken spine nicked the
spinal cord during all that movement, I could have
been paralyzed for life.

After I made it through the night and the first
uncertain weeks, Ed followed my progress
through our dentist, whom we both visited twice
yearly. He remained anonymous, feeling he didn't
deserve recognition for what other EMTs do
every day. But now it had been ten years, and he
felt we should meet.

When Ed finished his story, I laughed and cried
at the same time. At last I saw the evidence of
God's presence, and no one had to tell me about it.
I experienced it for myself, as if it had happened
that night!

The miraculousness of it all struck me. What
are the chances that a licensed EMT would drive
down the street the very moment I needed one?
That he would know the procedures to perform
and whom to call? That the call for help would go
out virtually the minute after the crash?

Sure, it was still secondhand; but the vividness
and authenticity with which Ed described the ex-

perience left no doubt in my mind: God had indeed performed a miracle to save my life on that eventful night. And Ed had showed up with his story at the Bible study so soon after my urgent "prayer." God gave me what I had asked for: a direct, conscious experience of God at work in my life! I was ashamed for thinking He had left me alone—He was there all the time!

Later that night, as I lay in bed, sleep wouldn't come because of my awe and gratitude, so I penned this poem:

HE CARES!
Your presence was a promise
My mind just couldn't share,
Until the night You proved to me
How very much You care.
How can I doubt that You are here?
For now I clearly see,
That when I really needed You,
You were always there for me!

ROBERT TREASH survived near-fatal injuries from a tragic accident that left him in a coma for months, then unable to walk or talk. With God's grace and the prayers of his friends and family, he not only regained these abilities but went on to finish college. He now serves with Wycliffe Bible Translators. Mr. Treash wrote this account of his experiences just before leaving for China for a one-year assignment teaching English as a second language. His permanent home is in Trumbull, Connecticut.

Ten Years in Africa (Ken-ya Believe It?)

Karen Y. Dace

As I lay in bed with yet another illness, my mind went back to when I first arrived in Kenya. I was there to begin my first assignment with Campus Crusade for Christ. It was January 1986 when I first set foot on Kenyan soil. I left winter in northern California to arrive in wonderful eighty-degree weather in Nairobi—a lovely Kenya summer.

My expectations were high. I wasn't sure just how I would be used, but I was eager to serve the Lord and make a difference in the lives of Kenyans. A new church was being started in Kileleshwa, an area of town with no church. I was asked to be a part of this new church. A week after I arrived, I began teaching a class of seven- to nine-year-old children, most of whom had never even seen a Bible or heard about Jesus Christ.

I'd never been away from home and family and I had never been seriously sick at any time before, so when I began to feel some stomach upset, I attributed it to adjustment. However, the pain persisted. It seemed that whatever illness was going around hit me hard and didn't go away.

I had asked God to draw me closer to Him, never expecting this would be His way. During my first several years in Kenya I continued to be plagued with illnessES—pinworm, hookworm, amoeba, shigella, heat rashes, an infected left eye, pains in my right arm and leg and a host of other problems. I began asking myself, *What in the world is God trying to teach me? Whatever it is, I wish I would hurry up and learn it.*

Each time I would get an illness, I would go to the same doctor for treatment. I would take the medicines faithfully, but it seemed I could not entirely cleanse my system of the problems.

When I developed an inner ear infection and serious throat infection, the throat infection progressed to an upper respiratory infection. I would cough so hard I would throw up. Whenever I ate, the same thing would happen. As long as I did not try to talk, I was ok. The chronic ear infection affected my equilibrium and the constant feeling of being unwell affected my spirit. I began sinking into depression.

I was asked to speak to a group of young professionals on the topic "Learning to Pray." I was still having problems with talking and breathing, but I wanted to give that presentation. I prayed that I would be able to speak for one hour without coughing. Not only was I able to speak for the whole time, but for some minutes beyond! The group asked many questions, and we had a wonderful time.

Although I had been faithfully reading my Bible, it seemed I had not let God's Word penetrate my heart. Then one day, as I was reading the familiar passage where Paul talks about buffeting his body and bringing it into subjection, these passages took on new and vital meaning for me, and I began to see a glimmer of hope in all my illnesses. An important truth was suddenly revealed to me. God wanted me to change my attitude—to rejoice and thank Him in the midst of my pain. I prayed that God would help me to do that.

I began to feel unwell again shortly after that time and went to the doctor for diagnosis and treatment. I was diagnosed with a serious case of typhoid fever and told to go home to California and stay there until I had recovered.

While making that diagnosis, the doctor also commented that my demeanor seemed different this visit. I could only smile when he said, "Before, you always came here complaining, with a negative spirit, but this time your whole attitude is different. Now you seem somehow to be accepting of the illness and more at peace with God."

There were some hard times during the typhoid fever—there was a question of whether I would recover—but the Lord brought me through and healed me. I returned to Africa after five months in the United States. It was good to be back. There is a saying that goes, "Once you drink of the waters of Africa, your thirst will not be quenched until you have returned once again." I can vouch for the truth of that statement.

Over the years, our little church in Kileleshwa grew rapidly. Now they have their own church building on their own plot of land, fully paid for. The Sunday school class of seven- to nine-year-olds has grown to over fifty children every week. More than twenty of these have become believers and are still following the Lord.

The church in Africa is considered to be one of the fastest-growing churches in the world today. It is reported that *every day* over 16,000 Africans convert to Christianity and a new denomination is started. What a blessing it is for me to be a part of this great work! I feel so privileged to be a recruit in God's army in Africa, working to finish this unfinished task and helping in the evangelization of the world.

In December 1995, we had our first student conference for all of Africa, Explo 95. I was asked to be the conference administrator, which was exciting and challenging. Seven hundred participants came and over half committed themselves to serving the Lord wherever He leads.

My work in Campus Crusade for Christ is now in the offices of the director of Southern and Eastern Africa Area (SEA). These offices have recently moved to Harare, Zimbabwe, and I am scheduled to leave for my new post in the fall of

1996. I will miss Kenya after ten years there, but I'm eager to serve the Lord wherever He wants me, and I look forward to blessings and adventures ahead in Zimbabwe.

What about my health? Praise the Lord, I'm healthy and strong again. There is a side effect of the typhoid fever that is usually permanent— short-term memory loss. But that cannot dim my gratitude for what the Lord has done for me. He has healed my body, and even more importantly, He has healed my spirit.

KAREN Y. DACE was born in Lebanon, Illinois and received her bachelor of arts degree from the University of California at Riverside. She spent ten years with Campus Crusade for Christ in Nairobi, Kenya, Africa, serving in various capacities, including continental accountant and executive secretary. She is currently serving as executive assistant to Campus Crusade's director for Southern and Eastern Africa (SEA). She is also pursuing a master's degree in finance. In September 1996, Karen, along with the SEA office, moved from Nairobi to Harare, Zimbabwe, where she continues working in service to the Lord.

A Distant Island

C. Christopher Knippers, Ph.D.

It was one of those halcyon days which seem to come along only about once a year. The air was crystal-clear, the sky a spectacular azure display. A gentle breeze caressed our sunlit faces as we gazed across a sparkling aqua sea from a palm bluff top in Laguna Beach. The love of my life, Gwen, was at my side—a gorgeous, kind, sophisticated young woman. We looked out toward an island twenty-five miles away and could see every crevice in the green hills of Santa Catalina.

All the stress of the years of graduate programs, internships and dissertation battles had melted away in that instant. I felt clearer and freer than I had ever felt in my entire life.

It had been a rough road to this place, but that was behind me now. I was looking in one direction—forward! I was standing on the threshold of a new era of total freedom and blessing, both in and through my life.

I was profoundly grateful to God. I had accomplished my goal of getting a Ph.D. in clinical psychology before the age of thirty; I had a wonderful fiancée; I was living where I wanted to live; I had dear old friends and exciting new friends; I was helping to start a dynamic new ministry; my lifelong dream of becoming a psychologist was coming true.

And I had the good health to enjoy all these blessings.

A few days later, I awoke in the morning surrounded by a dark fog. I struggled to figure out what was going on. I stumbled around the apartment. Outside the sun was shining brightly. But why was I seeing everything through a dark fog?

I dressed and went to my car to drive to my office for that morning's client appointments, then realized I couldn't do it. I went back to my apartment and sat in a stupor. Finally I called my sister Sue. She and my parents came right over, and after discussing the problem, we made an appointment with an ophthalmologist.

The surgeon examined me and said that my eyes had hemorrhaged internally. Capillaries in both eyes had burst for some unknown reason. He advised laser surgery to clear up the blood. But, with cold detachment, he added that the bleeding could return in the future and it was likely I would be blind within a few years.

I retreated into isolation for several days, rejecting attempts by family or friends to console me. I sank into deep despair. My mental and spiritual darkness exceeded the darkness of my physical vision. Fear and a sense of utter helplessness took over.

Had God abandoned me? Where was the God who had seemed so close as Gwen and I stood on the bluffs looking out at the island?

As I thought about that scene, an idea took shape. I would escape this torture and free my family and Gwen from the burden of caring for a helpless, bitter blind man. I would withdraw all my meager funds, buy a ticket to a South Pacific island, find a remote area and disappear from the earth—permanently. I felt so certain about this plan that I began getting my affairs in order.

I forced Gwen out of my life so that she would get on with her life and not be tied down by mine. I refused to answer the door or take her phone calls. I continued my preparations for a one-way trip to a distant island.

Until I could carry out the plan though, I decided I would undergo the laser surgery but with a different and more kindly surgeon. The surgery had to be performed without anesthesia, so it was painful and traumatic. As the first doctor had predicted, the blood cleared some and my vision was extended to about ten feet.

My despondency and desperation continued.

One night I was awakened by a brilliant light in my windowless bedroom. About ten feet away, I saw a woman sitting in my desk chair. She looked lovingly into my eyes, a slight smile on her face. She was luminous white with cascading hair, wearing a flowing luminous gown. I arose from

bed and walked over to her. She remained motionless and silent, gazing into my eyes with compassion.

I went to the sink and splashed cold water on
my face to make sure I was really awake, then returned to the bedroom. She was there exactly as
she had been before. I went back to bed, facing
her so I could see her loving face. She remained
motionless and silent, smiling, as I drifted back to
sleep.

When I awoke, I pondered the vision. I could
have dismissed it as a stress-induced hallucination,
as I'm sure many of my peers in psychotherapy
would have done. Instead, I chose to see it as a
sign that God was with me after all.

It was a small step of trust, but it was all I could
muster. The next day I noticed a lessening of the
fear and depression that had gripped me tighter
and tighter each day. My suicide plans faded into
memory; I knew I would never again nourish such
a thought, no matter what happened in my life. I
was still sad and had little hope for a bright future;
but now I had a renewed and growing trust in
God. I surrendered myself completely to God's
will. I trusted God with whatever happened, and
what's more, I wanted to stay around to see what
God was going to do next. I was interested in life
again.

The medical treatments continued. My surgeon, whom I had grown to trust, strongly recommended a radical new eye surgery. He sent me to
a surgeon of his choosing for a second opinion; the

latter emphatically agreed. I resigned myself to it, even though it would be a more complicated and traumatic surgery than I had previously experienced. I scheduled it for that week.

My parents, who had been supportive but uninvolved in my previous medical decisions, uncharacteristically opposed the planned surgery. They told me they felt uncomfortable about it and, as they prayed about it, became more convinced I should cancel the operation, at least temporarily.

I was angry at them for questioning what, for me, had been an agonizing personal decision. But they persisted, unintimidated by my anger. That caught my attention!

The clincher was a call from my aunt in Oklahoma, an aunt with whom I had never been close. She had heard about the radical surgery planned for me, had prayed for me and had made an appointment for me with a prominent eye surgeon in Los Angeles whom she knew personally. He was expecting me, she said, and would be able to tell me whether or not I should have the surgery.

That doctor examined me, then called in four world-acclaimed eye surgeons who "just happened" to be in Los Angeles that day for an international conference and lecture. All four concurred: There was absolutely no need for the high-risk procedure recommended by my doctor and his colleague.

Eventually I underwent another type of sur-

gery. The procedure, though painful, was successful; I was told that my eyesight would be just fine.

I learned years later that the surgeons actually
meant "fine" temporarily, not permanently as I
had assumed. I'm grateful they led me to believe
my vision was restored completely. That belief
helped it become a reality.

Now, ten years later, the doctor who assisted in
the surgery (a family friend) is still amazed by my
recovery. His professional card now reads, "The
doctor does the surgery, but God does the healing."

My eyesight is strong. I see clearly wearing con-
tact lenses with moderate correction. Slowly I
have come out of the despondency that weighed
me down for so long. I have a successful psychotherapy practice; I write books; I speak at workshops and seminars; I enjoy friends and family.

This experience has taught me some profound
truths about life:

1. "Blind trust" often precedes hope and
faith. You don't have to struggle to conjure
up faith in the midst of crisis. Just start with
simple, humble, childlike trust, and let
God's will work in your life.

2. Prayers of friends and relatives are extremely powerful in the process of healing.
Other people's faith can pull you through
even when yours is weak. It was not my

prayers but the prayers of others that began to turn my life around.

3. Recovery from trauma can be gradual and irregular. You must be persistent and determined. Often physical challenges are actually "spiritual battles" with a purpose and plan beyond our human understanding. Fight the battle, knowing that God is with you to empower and guide you! God just might send unlikely allies to help you, as happened in my case.

Find a place to go for inspiration, even if only in your mind. Go there often. I still go to that bluff looking out toward the island in the distance, and I remember God's promise of freedom and blessing.
I can see clearly now.

 C. CHRISTOPHER KNIPPERS, Ph.D., is a psychotherapist, speaker and the author of *Common Sense, Intuition, and God's Guidance*, with a psychotherapy practice in San Juan Capistrano and Laguna Beach, California. He is founding chairperson of the Mental Health Professional Network, a ministry of the National Association for Christian Recovery. He has also served as education director for Cancer Conquerors Foundation.

CHAPTER 9

BOUNCE BACK FROM
LOST FAITH

*I*t is not uncommon to hear strong, devout Christians confess to having gone through a period in their lives when they lost touch with God. In retrospect it would seem that this "doubting time" has somehow served to build a deeper, stronger faith. How these authors experienced and emerged victorious from their personal period of "wandering in the wilderness" is the powerful message of this chapter.

Fear not, for I have redeemed you; I have summoned you by name; you are mine. (Isaiah 43:1)

In Search of a Child

Jana Flaig

I thought God had forgotten me. Frank and I had been married for eleven years and had prayed for a child almost from the very beginning of our marriage, with no results.

After a few years of marriage, we started searching for a cure for our infertility. We tried surgeries, high-tech impregnation procedures and fertility treatments. Each procedure promised hope, but still I didn't get pregnant. Each time my hopes were crushed, and I was in despair.

Our pastor and friends prayed for us and prophecies were spoken to us that said we would have a child. With all that prayer and prophecy, we believed God would soon bless us with a child. But the months and years passed and still no child.

Frustration turned to anger and jealousy when I saw women pushing their babies in strollers in the

mall. *Why them and not me?* I kept asking myself—
and God. I stopped going to baby showers or visiting pregnant friends because envy seethed
within me. I dreaded going to church because of
the families with children all around me there.

Finally, after spending our life savings on infertility treatments, the pain of disappointment became greater than my desire to have a child. With
a mixture of anger and sadness, I told Frank,
"This pain is too much for me. I can't stand it any
more. Let's stop trying. The Lord doesn't seem to
care." We gave up.

Neither Frank nor I were accustomed to failure.
We both have been blessed with success in other
areas of our lives. I was a television news reporter
before becoming a college instructor and professional speaker. My husband Frank Brummett is a
successful attorney.

"I guess the Lord has another plan for us,"
Frank said gently. "In any event, we have to leave
it to Him."

For years, I wouldn't consider adoption because
I believed God wanted us to have a child who was
biologically our own. Then a couple who are our
close friends went to China to adopt a baby. I was
skeptical until they returned home with a cuddly,
healthy three-month-old baby girl.

As my friend Celeste told me how happy they
were with the baby and how the foreign adoption process worked, I felt God changing my
hardened heart about adoption. It had taken
God twelve years and just an instant to make me

see adoption (especially *foreign* adoption) in a whole new light.

Eagerly, Frank and I visited Bal Jaget Children's World in Chatsworth, California, the agency that had handled our friends' adoption. They said it was quite likely we could have a baby within a year. We had heard "no" so many times, it was thrilling to hear this "yes."

We met with families who had adopted abroad. They explained that foreign adoptions have fewer restrictions and are faster than domestic adoptions. Parents usually wait six to twelve *months* for a foreign adoption, compared with one to five years in the U.S.

But, they warned us, the road would be expensive and difficult. In addition to paying for mountains of paperwork, we would have to travel to the country of the child's birth. In addition to bureaucratic uncertainties, there were state adoption laws, federal immigration laws and the laws of the foreign country that had to be dealt with.

Undeterred by the threat of these complexities, Frank and I threw ourselves into preparation for parenthood. We opted for a Russian baby because we wanted a child who looked like us. Frank tried to learn conversational Russian in a hurry. I decorated the nursery with Disney wallpaper and a bright red crib. We told friends, "It's Moscow meets Mickey Mouse at our house now."

One early spring day in 1994, we received a

video tape from Moscow. We popped it into the
player and saw a baby boy lying naked on a table.

His skin was milky white, his limbs thin, his
belly distended. He was three months old and
weighed eight pounds, about the weight of a newborn in the United States. His large round eyes
appeared hollow, but they eagerly followed the
movement of a rattle shaken before his face.

I prayed for a sign that this child was meant to
be ours. We studied the little boy's face. I can't tell
you exactly what I saw, but I recognized something in his face that said he was *our* son. And besides, he had red hair; I had always wanted a
red-haired child.

We left for Moscow later that month. God went
along and opened all the doors for us, providing
the money that was needed for processing and
travel, even untangling the usual red tape to make
our way smooth and easy.

A Russian guide arranged our stay in a tiny
apartment during the adoption proceedings. She
lectured us: "Foreign adoptions in Russia are legal, but the public does not approve. Keep to
yourselves. Do not take the baby out except to
meet with the officials who must approve the
adoption. To avoid muggers, don't speak English in public."

The next day we went to the orphanage, knowing God was with us. On that freezing day in
March, we met our son. I had dreamed of this moment and wondered what it would feel like. I

thought I might cry, but no tears came. I had expected stress, but felt calm and at peace.

"He's beautiful," I whispered, bending over to kiss him on his forehead.

We felt God's presence as we spent the next few days getting acquainted with our new son in the bleak apartment now filled with light and joy. Finally the day came when we took our baby to appear before the Chief of Adoptions. Her final words to us will stay in our hearts for as long as we live: "This orphan will now have a good life. Russia gives you her son."

At that moment a Russian orphan called Sasha became Luke Flaig-Brummett, the son we had waited for for so long and traveled halfway around the world to claim as ours.

I made one last entry in the journal I kept while in Moscow: "I cried because it's over. The pain, the anger and the longing for a child all these years is over. And the last year—the nightmare of paperwork, the stress and uncertainty of the adoption process—is over. I have a son."

Luke, now a lively two-year-old, is ahead of the growth curve for his age. With his reddish-blond flat top, sparkling blue eyes and friendly "high fives," he comes across as a miniature "cool dude."

Now we know God didn't forget us after all. He had Luke in mind with every pregnancy test I failed. Yes, God had another plan in mind—a beautiful plan for Frank, for me and for Luke.

JANA FLAIG, M.A., former TV news on-camera reporter and assignment editor in Los Angeles, is a college professor and professional speaker specializing in helping those who want a child realize their dream through international adoption. She has personal experience in foreign adoption, preceded by twelve years of failed infertility treatments. She and her husband live in Orange County, California with their son Luke. Jana is a member of the National Speakers Association.

God Doesn't Let You Go

Terry L. Paulson, Ph.D.

I once visited a theological seminary and, for a long time afterward, I struggled to recover my sense of joy. —Norman Vincent Peale

Those unsettling words from Norman Vincent Peale ring true in describing the darkest days in my walk with God. For many believers called to serve, their time at seminary is a time of nurturing and an opportunity for deepening their faith. In some ways for me it was that but, as I studied both the precepts of my faith and the principles of my emerging profession as a psychologist, my faith took a back seat to my struggle to understand and control God.

Even though I searched and studied diligently for understanding, I expected that surely at a

seminary God would give me a deeper faith and
growth in grace. Instead, the joy and the simple
faith that had served me as a young man gave way
to intellectual one-upmanship. Assertive psycholo-
gists trying to make their mission and message
relevant and threatened theology faculty trying to
solidify their place of power in the seminary hier-
archy played volleyball with my mind. I left seminary six years later with every degree I had
pursued, but with a deep disillusionment and a
faith in hibernation.

Not all of our spiritual struggles as Christians
require bouncing back from external tragedies or
crippling losses. Sometimes one's most difficult
challenges come from within. In the ensuing years
I would come to learn a very important lesson: As
we journey through the valley of the shadow of
life in the fast lane, even when we think we are
doing fine alone, God does not forsake His sheep.

I sublimated my disillusionment and spiritual
conflict by reaching out for the "good life" or, as
we used to say, "going for the gusto." The specif-
ics of my fall would be hard to see for those
watching on the sidelines of my life. On the surface, things went well. Already used to poverty in
school, it was the best time to start my own company. After all, I had little to lose and a dream I
believed I could achieve. Riding the hot topic of
assertiveness, our company and profits grew. The
balance sheet took a turn to the positive as my
counseling clients gave way to speaking to associations and corporations throughout the country. I

had made a name for myself, and I had made it without God—or so I thought.

Yet something was missing. I would certainly not have admitted it to anyone, much less myself. While I played the game of life as I knew it, God walked silently beside me, patiently waiting for me to return to the fold.

Even on the sidelines, evidence of problems were beginning to show. There was a divorce that shocked my family and friends. As I tried to pull my life back together, going to church was not part of the answer. I was a psychologist and an assertive one at that. I was sure that I could take care of my own life without any help from man or God.

I stayed busy as a full-time speaker and trainer, a part-time dad and a budding lover to my new wife-to-be. The money was tighter, but I was happier. I knew I could be successful, and it wasn't too many years before my accountant confirmed that it was true. I had made it. In my mind there was no need for God.

But the Good Shepherd knows His sheep, and for that one lost sheep He would wait. . . .

Soon we were in our new home and my speaking career was blossoming. My accomplishments were even beginning to match what I said in my brochures!

On one trip, after speaking to a 3,000-person audience in Minneapolis, I called home between planes. My wife had a little surprise.

"I hope you're sitting down," Lorie said with a

smile in her voice. "I got a little surprise dropped off today. Your son is here to live with us."

Yes, my ten-year-old son, whom we had seen regularly on weekends and for more extended times on vacations, was doing more than just visiting. He had decided to live with us.

I have only respect for my ex-wife's wisdom in letting him make that choice; it could not have been easy for her to do. For Lorie and me there were moments of joy, concerns, new plans and many new responsibilities. No more part-time parents; he was here for the long haul. God's lost sheep had all of a sudden taken on a herd.

In fact, little did I know that it was through Sean that God would reach out to touch both myself and my wife.

Like many Americans caught up in the good life, for us Sunday church just never seemed important enough to attend. Maybe if they had made every day Easter we might have made a point of attending. For Lorie and me, Sunday was a day we could sleep in, go for a long run or do a 10K race.

But Sean changed all that. We now had an emerging teenager on our hands. How did we cope? We did what every panicked new parent does—we did what our parents did! We decided to take him to church to get a good grounding. To us, whether God joined us there was not essential; we would settle for the good grounding.

The Good Shepherd was opening a gate to the pasture he had been preparing for us.

There were churches visited, but not felt. There were weekends when our Sunday road race made attending any church out of the question. After all, it was a good-looking T-shirt, and what we were doing was for our health.

But one Sunday, with no race to run, we found our way to Westlake Lutheran Church. We felt the smiles, the outstretched hands and the warm appeal of a minister who obviously cared. There is that great gospel song, "You're the Only Jesus Some Will Ever See." How true it was for us that day! Jesus came to us through Eileen Green, Mary Ann Fiore, even Pastor Lawson himself.

Jesus touched us anew that Sunday. Sean wanted to go back and so did we.

The Body of Christ in the world relies on the strengths of Christians to minister and serve. Little did I realize that no sooner had we begun attending our new church than God called Lorie and me to serve Him. For it turned out that Westlake Lutheran had no youth group. If the church was to meet our needs, it had to have a youth group. And a youth group would need a director.

Having someone right there with over ten years of youth director experience, stacks of programs ready to go and a somewhat crazy and funny personality that seemed more like a perpetual teenager than a psychologist, God, it seemed, had but one logical choice—me. I don't know whether I opened my mouth, raised my hand or nodded my head, but one part of my body betrayed me when the pastor asked who would take on the job.

Soon, Lorie and I were immersed in kids. We had agreed to minister, but they ended up ministering to us. I am convinced that to work with teens you have to have a sense of humor and be authentic. The humor was a given; the Spirit had to work overtime on the authentic part.

It wasn't as hard as one might think. I was letting go and letting God work through me. Instead of searching for the right theological or psychological answers, I was trusting God to provide. Simple prayers and long-forgotten verses touched my soul again. Both Lorie and I were now feeling God's presence in our lives. There were *deja vu* moments of a ministry long since passed that were now again coming to life.

Over the years of working with youth, there were many moments of joy, hundreds of programs, many retreats, songs sung and service projects completed. My son is now married and out on his own. Many of "our kids" from those early groups have taken the same path, but they remain "our kids." God has blessed us with the sounds of laughter and tears, with hugs of joy and comfort, with opportunities to serve and to grow. God has indeed been faithful.

I have not looked at my notes from seminary since I left, but I have claimed the fruit of the Spirit in my daily walk. I have also come to understand that God sometimes helps us to bounce back when we do not even know we are lost. For as Jesus said of the Good Shepherd in John 10:3: "The sheep listen to his voice. He calls his own sheep by name." You and I have been called by name. We are His. He will not fail or forsake us. Draw near to Him for He is always near you.

> *Fear not, for I have redeemed you; I have summoned you by name; you are mine.*
>
> *When you pass through the waters, I will be with you; and when you pass through the rivers, they will not sweep over you. When you walk through the fire, you will not be burned; the flames will not set you ablaze. . . . Since you are precious and honored in my sight, and because I love you. . . . Do not be afraid, for I am with you. (Isaiah 43:1-2, 4-5)*

TERRY L. PAULSON, Ph.D., is a licensed psychologist, professional speaker and author of four books: *Paulson on Change; They Shoot Managers, Don't They?; Making Humor Work;* and *Secrets of Life Every Teen Should Know.* He conducts programs for large corporations and has made presentations to numerous hospitals, universities, churches and associations throughout the U.S. *Business Digest* called him "the Will Rogers of management consultants." That humorous, down-to-earth style has also served him well as a youth leader. He resides in Agoura Hills, California.

A Cry in the Night

Jan Northington

"Welcome aboard Flight 703, departing Orange County to San Jose." The flight attendant's words barely registered as I stared at the seat in front of me. My three-year-old daughter was in the seat next to me while I held my six-month-old son.

I must be dreaming, I said to myself, slumping in my seat. I hadn't slept for thirty-six hours. Why wouldn't my eyes shut? The pressure of my swollen lids reminded me of my frequent tears the past few weeks. I felt smothered by despair, hungering for a breath that would satisfy my thirst for air. My body ached, my head throbbed and I fought nausea.

"If there should be a loss in cabin pressure, the masks above you will drop. . . ." the attendant piped. The distant words squeezed into the ones my mind kept going over and over.

This isn't happening to me. What will my parents think when I tell them? Can I say my husband needed a little time to himself? I knew the truth. He wasn't happy in our marriage and wanted distance to decide its value.

Fresh tears blurred the runway lights. I felt a tugging on my sleeve. "Why do we have to wear seat belts?" my daughter questioned. "Can I have a drink of water? When will the plane go?"

I turned my head toward her innocent smile. What had she said? . . . Seat belts . . . a drink . . . plane?

I shook my head, "Not now, honey."

The pressures of the past few years have just caught up with him, I reasoned. *It's only a phase. He'll work it out. The best thing I can do is give him a week free from the demands of the children.*

The starting of the plane's engine brought another tug on my sleeve. "Are we going, Mama?"

"Yes, honey, soon."

I'll bet being alone will show him how much he wants and needs his family. When I get back, we'll start a new life together. I held those comforting thoughts as we began to taxi the runway.

A flight attendant broke into my reflections. "You may want to give your baby something to suck on when we take off," she said. Mechanically, I pulled a bottle of juice from my bag and slipped it in my son's mouth.

The engine roared louder as the plane gained momentum. My baby sucked like a starfish being pried from a rock. My daughter squeezed my limp hand and grinned with excitement. I forced a smile for her.

As the plane took flight, I was suddenly flooded with fear. *Someone was missing! Where was my husband?* I felt like standing in the aisle screaming, "Help! I'm all alone!"

My eyes burned as tears dripped off my chin. I whisked away the tears with the back of my sleeve. I couldn't let my children see their mother falling apart.

"Let's sing a song, Mommy," my daughter begged. In a joyful, high-pitched voice, she began, "Jesus loves me, this I know, for the Bible tells me so."

As if they were stones, I began throwing those words at God. *You love me, huh? You've caused me to hurt like this—is that Your love? And what about this morning?*

The scene had played repeatedly in my mind. After working all night as a nurse, I got home at 7 a.m. to be met by my husband's announcement, "I can't watch the children today while you sleep." He stared at the floor, a sad look on his face. He looked more than his thirty years.

"I don't have the patience I need to care for them. I need to leave the house, go somewhere, anywhere."

My heart raced and my voice trembled as I offered, "What would you think if I took the children to my parents for a week or so? It might give you the time and space you need to sort things out."

"Good idea. I know the children will be happier there than seeing me like this. I'd like to talk to the pastor, and maybe it would be better if I spoke to him alone." Quickly, he kissed the children and left.

Had I been abandoned on this morning? The past few weeks my husband had grown distant. Something had come between us, but it remained a complete mystery. Day after day of rejection had brought confusion, despair, sleeplessness. Leaning my head on the headrest, I realized that today, for the first time in nearly a decade, I didn't know where my husband was. He didn't know if I had actually gone to my parents. Did he even care?

"Aren't airplanes fun, Mommy?"

"Oh, yes, honey."

Surely he would call my parents' house when he found us gone. Surely he'd want to know if we had arrived safely. I felt relief knowing that I could count on certain things after so many years together.

"Let's sing again, Mommy!"

Anything to pass the time and keep these children happy, I thought.

"Yes, Jesus loves me. Yes, Jesus loves me. The Bible tells me so."

Once again, I talked back to God. *So the Bible tells me You love me, huh? If that's Your love I'm feeling now, You can go shower it on someone else.*

Had an hour passed? The flight attendant again suggested, "You may want to give your baby something to suck on. We're getting ready to land." I pulled out a second bottle, buckled in my daughter and held my baby tightly. Suddenly I felt a weight of responsibility I'd never known.

I'm all alone! I'll have to make every decision alone.

During the drive to my parents' house, little was said, but after settling the children in bed, I felt my parents deserved an explanation.

I was so tired I thought, *I can't talk, think or explain anything until I get some sleep. I'll tell them in the morning.*

But I stood there rooted to the floor. Mom sank into her chair, her eyes filled with tears. My dad came over and hugged me tightly. We sobbed together. I couldn't remember a time my dad displayed such deep emotion.

I couldn't go to sleep. I kept struggling to figure things out and beat off the fears that overwhelmed me. *What was to become of my future?* I wondered. *Our future? Our children? Our home? Our jobs? Was my whole world falling apart?*

I shook my fist at the ceiling and reminded God of the injustice of my situation, reminded Him that He promised to be there when everyone else vanished. Though I didn't feel any love at that moment, I kept thinking of a verse that said, "Never will I leave you; never will I forsake you" (Hebrews 13:5). The words played over and over in my mind.

Was this the time to take God at His word? Could I commit my life to something I could not feel? Could I believe God's love would be so trustworthy that He would stand with me, no matter what happened?

I sobbed, "Oh God, please help me sleep. Help me think. Help me care for my kids, make the right choices. Help me follow You. I have nothing to offer You . . . except me. I feel so weak, scared, rejected, unloved. Whatever You want from me, You've got it. No one else wants me, it seems. If You want me, I'm Yours."

The phone never rang. My pillow was drenched. My eyes stung, but I drifted off to a peaceful, solid sleep. I awoke with a clear and un-shakable faith to call my own. His words, "Never will I leave you; never will I forsake you," have never left me since that decisive night.

Months later, while sipping coffee with a friend, she asked, "Where does your joy come from in the midst of such pain?"

I answered with the assurance that my prayer had become a reality. I declared, "It's Jesus! He's become everything to me! Any joy you see is the result of His peace. Not peace because my cir-cumstances are easy; they're not. I have peace be-cause I know God is faithful, even in the light of others' unfaithfulness!"

Hesitating, she countered, "But how do you trust someone you can't even see?"

Her question interrupted my reflection of what a nightmare the past few months would have been had I not chosen to trust God and His promise. I was mindful that God was not threatened by my honest questions, weak faith or accusations. He merely loved me just as He promised and brought wholeness to my broken life.

"You can see Him! He's reflected in nature . . . in people . . . in people who have no logical reason to be joyful."

As I continue waiting to see the final direction of my marriage, I may cry a thousand more tears. The pain of my first plane ride might come again, but never—never again—will I be alone.

Taken from *Separated and Waiting* by Jan Northington © 1994 Thomas Nelson Publishing. Used by permission.

JAN NORTHINGTON is a freelance writer and conference speaker, trained and promoted through Christian Leaders, Authors and Speakers Services (CLASS), Inc. She is the author of the book, *Separated and Waiting* (Thomas Nelson, 1994) and has written numerous articles for the Christian marketplace. Jan resides in Los Osos along the central coast of California with her husband and four children.

CHAPTER 10

BOUNCE BACK MORE THAN ONCE

*H*ave you ever felt like saying, "Lately my life is one bad thing after another. I feel like I must be wearing a 'Kick Me' sign"? Perhaps you have prayed, read Scripture and surrendered your problems to the Lord and yet your troubles keep coming. It's hard to understand why God does not intervene. God allowed Job's faith to be tested and, for His own reasons, He sometimes allows ours to be tested too. Each author in this chapter has had to bounce back more than once, but each one persevered and trusted in God's strength and wisdom through the dark times. As a result, God has blessed their lives.

Transformation: Deep Pain into Great Joy

Betty J. Price

Life was good—I had an affectionate husband, a son and a daughter, a country home with a white picket fence and family life that included praying together and attending church regularly.

This "great American dream" abruptly ended in horror the morning I approached the childrens' room and found my baby girl dangling from her crib. I rushed into the room to remedy the problem but soon detected a lifeless body. Somehow she had slipped between the mattress and netting of her crib and had been spun around and around repeatedly. In the moments that followed my husband and I carefully cut the cord from her neck and frantically tried to breathe life back into this precious little body, but to no avail.

Sorrow became a way of life. In the midst of

our emotional struggle, we could not bear the
thought of a courtroom battle with the company
that manufactured this new technology crib, but
did find some consolation in their immediate re-
moval of it from the market based on our letter.
Our failure to work through grief in a manner that
would draw us closer together caused unhealthy
repercussions. Nothing helped, including the birth
of another child far too soon after little Pam's
death. The marriage deteriorated rapidly until I
felt complete despair.

At one point, I felt I had reached the end of my
rope. After all, I'd been told daily for many
months that I was a bad mother and I was convinced that God couldn't love me if I left my marriage, so what good reason was there to continue
living? I even retrieved a gun from the office safe
with intentions of ending my misery, but then
changed my mind.

To this day I believe it was only the hand of
God that prevented me from using that gun. It
was about this time that my parents, who had
never before interfered in my adult life, inter-
vened and insisted that the boys and I leave this
abusive environment and stay with them for a
while, which I did. I was soon out on my own,
working and providing for the needs of a single-
parent home.

In spite of feeling that God couldn't love me in
my unwanted situation, I decided to continue
making church an important part of my life—the
alternative was unacceptable! This choice precipi-

tated an interest in music, beginning with an invitation to sing in the choir. Shortly thereafter, I was asked if I'd be interested in joining the handbell choir (at the time I didn't even know what a handbell was). In addition, I enjoyed attending a monthly Audrey Meier singalong over the hill from where I lived. I always arrived late because of my work schedule and sat in the back, but that didn't keep Audrey Meier's love from reaching across all those seats and touching my heart. Though I didn't believe it was a possibility for me, I thought: *I wish I could love others and touch their lives the way that lady does.* Little did I realize that this involvement with music would become so significant for me in the years ahead.

The hope of rebuilding a better life was short-lived when my oldest son was in a major accident. He needed specialized care that required the signature of both parents. His father agreed to provide the needed medical help only if the child lived with him. Since he had remarried a wonderful Christian lady who'd been a high school friend and they were active in church, I acquiesced—there seemed to be no other option available.

Though it was difficult, I knew I *must* rise above my own pain for the sake of my youngest son. I did my best to lessen his grief, but the loss of his brother was too much for him to bear. In about a year the school psychologist called to discuss the importance of arranging for my son to visit his brother. So it was that he went for Christmas but never came back.

With resources that barely took care of our needs, there again seemed to be nothing I could do except love my sons enough to be willing to allow them to live in what I believed was a loving Christian home.

My life was crumbling with no apparent escape from a deep hole of depression. I realized that my parents loved me, but they were on the mission field, unavailable by phone or dependable mail service. As you might imagine, I embarked on a *huge* pity party. One Sunday morning I ran out of church in tears feeling like Humpty Dumpty. I was sure that the shattered pieces of my life could never be put back together again. An observant assistant pastor followed, caught me by the shoulder and said, "I don't know if I can do anything to change your situation but I do know that I *care!*" For hours I cried so hard that I felt turned inside-out, but I could not escape those two words: *"I care."*

My pastor had tried to help me understand that God doesn't withhold His love for any reason. For months I pored over the Scriptures every evening after work to see if this was true.

Once I understood and accepted that I was cared about, I had an overwhelming desire to care about others. For starters, I volunteered in a nursing home doing little things to bring some sunshine into the residents' lives. Little by little a transformation was occurring. I discovered that I *did* have the capacity to love others. And the more I cared about others, the greater my joy became.

Over several years, this eventually led to a "choirchimes" music ministry with an emphasis on touching lives. This metamorphosis began with hearing *I care*—those words were the catalyst that enabled me to become the kind of woman the little girl inside of me always hoped I'd grow up to be.

BETTY J. PRICE is the author of the book *101 Ways to Fix Broccoli*. She has also written numerous articles and is the owner of *Customized Funding Services,* a company that provides no-debt cash flow solutions to businesses. Betty also has a unique music ministry as a soloist for churches and retirement homes on instruments called "Choirchimes," which are similiar to handbells. She lives in San Diego, California.

Let God Take the Reins

Jennifer Botkin Phillips

"Jennifer, do you want to go horseback riding?" twelve-year-old Mary asked as we walked along the shore of Lake Huron in Red Bay, Canada.

"Gosh, I'd love to," I replied, remembering happy times of riding when I attended summer camp many years ago and thousands of miles away in the Sierra Nevada mountains.

The crisp air and sparkling lake at Red Bay reminded me of that summer when I was Mary's age and I went horseback riding every chance I got. I remembered picking the same chestnut brown horse every day and pretending he was my very own.

Now here I was at a perfect place to go riding again. My friend Mary Jane had invited me to join her and her family at their vacation cottage in Canada. At first I declined, thinking the offer was too kind and the timing was wrong for me, but Mary Jane insisted. "It will be just the thing for you," she said, tactfully alluding to a series of tragedies and traumas that had recently befallen me. It seemed Mary Jane may have been right. I was starting to feel a little better.

The following Monday, Mary Jane dropped her daughter Mary and me at the Purple Valley Riding Stables while she went to town to run errands. Right away, I noticed a chestnut brown quarter horse.

"That's the one I want," I told our trail guide, Dwight. "What's her name?"

"Foxy Lady," he answered in a lilting Canadian accent.

"This is going to be such fun!" I said gleefully.

Mary picked a handsome dark brown horse named Shadow. We were helped into our saddles, given a few tips on holding the reins and off we went, trailing after Dwight for our one-hour ride through the Canadian countryside.

I was thrilled at the opportunity to visit one of the Great Lakes and proudly wore my new cap that said "Canada" across the top. The wind swayed the birch trees as we rode beside stream beds and past fields of wildflowers. When we came to a meadow, we found ourselves bouncing along as Dwight led our horses in a trot. We broke out in giggles of laughter. I tried pushing my feet down in the stirrups, but it wasn't a smooth ride and I had to grip the saddle horn to stay atop.

How did the cowboys ever manage out on the range? I

wondered. Dwight said he would be starting a five-day ride the next day. *Five days on a horse!* But of course those people would be experienced riders—not like me, who only went riding about once every ten years.

We wound up the trail with only the rustling of the tall grass and the symphony of the birds as background music. It was peaceful, and I began to reflect on the turbulent events of the past few months. The previous December I'd lost my job and then in January started my own business and also began making contacts in an effort to resume my radio talk show. Two months later, my husband of six years walked out, and only a few days after that, my brother had abdominal hemorrhaging and went home to be with the Lord. It was all so overwhelming—too much for one person to handle.

The final straw had dropped while I was driving up to Red Bay. My car broke down on the New York Thruway just south of Niagara Falls. It turned out the transmission was broken. I called Mary Jane and her husband Mike, who suggested I leave the car there and let the mechanic try to sell it, which I did. Mary Jane drove four hours to pick me up.

Despite all this, I found myself relaxing as the horses carried us along the trail. I could understand why Mary Jane loved Red Bay. Each morning, we took mugs of steaming coffee out to her garden, where we sat on a bench and read from a devotional book. We sat among rows of phlox, iris, daisies and day lilies, seeking God's direction for our lives. In the evenings, we watched the magnificent Canadian sunsets on Lake Huron, peace and serenity filling our spirits. With God's handiwork all around, I was finding the rest and restoration my soul so desperately needed.

My calm thoughts halted suddenly as I realized that Dwight's horse was galloping. Then Mary's horse started to gallop. I wanted to shout, "Wait, Dwight, I don't think I should be galloping!" but it was too late. Foxy Lady had followed the others and was galloping while I hung on for dear life, shouting, "Whoa! Whoa! Slow down, Foxy Lady! Dwight! Oh! I don't think I should be gallop—"

Thud. "Ouch!" I'd fallen on my back just a few feet from some rocks and trees. "Mary . . ." I moaned, "I can't breathe. Oh . . . my back!"

Within seconds Dwight and Mary were at my side, calming and comforting me. Dwight offered to ride back to the stable to get a pickup truck, or I could *try* to get back on my horse. Neither was appealing, but I was having some trouble breathing, and I didn't want him to leave me, so I chose to ride back to the stable. By the time we got there, I was in excruciating pain. Mary Jane was there waiting for us and she took me immediately to the emergency room of the local hospital where I spent the night. The next day, I was discharged and told that I had a fracture in my back. I was instructed to rest and take pain pills as necessary.

Initially I had planned to stay at the cottage with Mary Jane and her family for only ten days.

Now they suggested I stay for the remainder of their vacation and ride back to New Jersey with them at the end of the month. At first I wanted to get home as soon as possible. I kept thinking, *I've got to check my mail, make follow-up phone calls and send out more résumé letters to radio stations.*

But a few days later, as I lay in pain on the couch, the reality of my crisis began to sink in. Not only was I not able to drive, but I had no car! It was broken and had been left in Batavia, New York! And now I was broken too and lay with a fractured back that could take months to heal.

I don't have time to be incapacitated, I argued within myself. I had no job, no car, no money, no husband and now no health or strength. I was flat on my back and looking up. Talk about hailing a cab; I needed to hail an angel! *Lord, don't You know I have to make a living?* I pleaded.

But thoughts of God's many unexpected blessings also began to fill my mind as I lay recovering at Red Bay. I remembered the time someone left four bags of groceries on my doorstep with fresh flowers and a note that read, "Remember, Jennifer, God loves you and He will provide." I thought of last Christmas when the daughter of a dear friend sent $100 toward the computer I needed.

A Scripture verse I had claimed years earlier came rushing back to my mind: "We are afflicted in every way, but not crushed; perplexed, but not driven to despair; persecuted, but not forsaken; struck down, but not destroyed" (2 Corinthians

4:8-9, RSV). That verse had strengthened and sustained me many years earlier when I was the victim of a violent crime. Now I tucked it into my heart once again with a prayer that it would fortify me to face my future unafraid.

I had come to Red Bay to retreat from my problems, but God had restoration of mind and soul for me there. As I continuously focused on His promise that I am *not forsaken or destroyed,* I grew more and more confident, and I am still holding on to that confidence, that I *shall* bounce back in the future, just as I have in the past. I only need to let go and let God take the reins.

JENNIFER BOTKIN PHILLIPS, author of *Nice Girls Don't Get Raped* and president of JBP Media Relations, is a member of Toastmasters International and the New York Tri-State National Speakers Association. She is also a graduate of CLASS (Christian Leaders, Authors and Speakers Seminars), Inc. Jennifer has taught adult education for over ten years and presents seminars on a corporate and community level. She lives in Park Ridge, New Jersey.

All Regrets, All Forgiven

Katie Phelps

I remember the day as if it were only yesterday. The long Thanksgiving weekend was about to begin. I started packing my things. I grabbed a few casual clothes, a few work clothes and my toiletries—that was all. I loaded my car without allowing myself to think too much. I was scared. I had never gone on a trip like the one I was about to take. This was not just any other day. It was the day I walked out on Tom, my husband.

The feeling of numbness that came over me was like nothing I had ever experienced. It felt as though someone were dying. Perhaps someone was.

I could not understand how the separation of two people could hurt so desperately. After all, I rationalized, we were only married for one year, and being together had made us both so miserable. I remember thinking during that trying time, *What have I done?* And now, despite the agonizing pain of separation, from where I stood on that gloomy fall day I saw no other choice but to end our marriage.

As time passed, I tried to find my way in the new and exciting life I had chosen for myself. I found a new job, a new car, a new apartment. I discovered new music, new friends, new relationships. *All I need now is a new husband,* I thought. I was certain I would find one, the right one, who could bring me the happiness that I self-righteously felt I deserved.

Despite the excitement and novelty of the life I was now living, I realized that something was missing, something I knew in my heart I truly needed: a closer walk with God. As a result, I privately committed my new, messed up life to God.

For me this was a new beginning. Things began to change. I started attending a strong, biblically based church and even committed myself to a weekly Bible study. There I met a group of people much different from any I had known at the church of my youth. These people seemed to have something I didn't have—and I wanted it! But what was it? Somehow, I felt distanced from them.

I could not yet see how my pride kept me at a distance from God. I had continually refused to commit my life publicly at the many altar calls I had attended. It seemed unnecessary to me. I believed in Jesus. I knew that He died for my sins. I saw no need to make public what was plainly a private pact between God and myself.

Then an amazing thing happened. After listening to a study on the Ten Commandments, I realized the inconceivable. In God's eyes, Tom and I were still married and, if I were to remarry, I would be knowingly commiting adultery. I was horrified! But oh, how it all made sense to me then—the constant worries about Tom and his well-being, the aching to tell him of all my regrets, the longing to have him hold me again. No wonder my heart felt ripped in two. And poor Tom— the pain he must have felt—was unbearable to me now. I heard the Scripture as if for the first time where Jesus said, "Therefore what God has joined together, let man not separate" (Matthew 19:6), and I realized that by leaving Tom I had acted in disobedience to God's Word. Why had I not known this before?

But what could I do now? It had been three years since I left Tom, with not so much as a phone call between us. I did not even know where he lived. *Oh Lord, help me! I was wrong and I am sorry!* I wanted so desperately to apologize that I did the only thing I could do—I wrote Tom a letter and prayed it would reach him through his mother who still lived nearby.

It was the most difficult letter of my life for one reason only—regret. I prayed Tom would sense my love for him after all these years and that he could begin to forgive me for being such an unloving wife. The love I had shown Tom was selfish and brassy, controlling and immature. The love I felt for him now was different. In my letter, I said he would always be my husband, and there had not been and would never be anyone who could take his place. In a final leap of faith, I included my phone number. Then I waited.

A few months passed. In some ways I was relieved that I had not heard from Tom. Could I lovingly take him back into my life? There had been much ugliness and pain between us, and I still carried the emotional scars of his volatile temper and cruel words. But I rested on the Lord's promise that His will would be done.

Then God did the almost unbearable. For one month He laid Tom so heavily on my heart that it ached. I could not shake the certainty that Tom was hurting deeply. Somehow, I felt his pain. The overwhelming concern I felt for him frightened me more than I can describe. I kept coming back to the same question, *God, are You trying to tell me to go back to Tom?* Was it possible Tom had changed? I had to know.

Tom's mother was more than surprised to hear my voice on the phone. Was Tom all right? Had he read my letter? She tried to reassure me Tom was finally happy—she thought. But her confession that she seldom spoke to him confirmed what my heart had been telling me: Tom had *not* changed for the better and he was hurting deeply.

About this same time, I was given an opportunity to serve as a follow-up counselor for a local evangelistic crusade. During the training session my eyes were directed, oddly enough, to a banner displaying the dates the crusade would be held in Tom's town. Immediately, I sent off an invitation to the crusade with this simple note: "Dear Tom, I pray that you will go to this and bring a friend. It changed my life. Love, Katie."

And pray I did. God was the only one who could free Tom from the guilt, pain and depression that continued to haunt him throughout his life.

Still my heart could not find peace. The ominous feeling I had about Tom oppressed me so that I cried out one night in prayer, "God, I will give You two more weeks. If You want me to go back to Tom, show me. If not, please let this hurt end, because I cannot live the rest of my life this way. Amen." Out of sheer desperation, I turned it over to Him once and for all.

The following week I learned that my pastor would be baptizing new believers. Without remembering my prayer, I knew this was my opportunity to be obedient and finally make public my commitment to Christ. As my pastor lifted me from beneath the ocean water, I had an overwhelming desire to tell him about my divorce. I sobbed my unforgiveness of myself, but he graciously cut me short and replied, "What divorce?"

I was stunned. My sins had been forgiven. God had washed away every last wrong from my past, including my decision to leave Tom. Then it hit me. It was exactly two weeks earlier when I had

prayed for God to give me a sign, and this was it!
I was free! Free from guilt! Free from regret! I
will never forget the feeling of freedom and total
joy that enveloped me that beautiful September
16th.

My life from that day forward took on a new
light. I now knew the meaning of true forgiveness.
I now understood what I had been missing in my
Christian walk—true humbleness. He answered
my pitiful prayer with more goodness and gra-
ciousness than I could ever imagine, and I knew
that my life would never be the same.

Little did I know then how much my life was to
be changed on that memorable September day.
The phone call came two weeks later. My heart
knew the truth even before it was spoken. The
Lord had somehow prepared me. Tom had taken
his life on September 16th—the day of my baptism.

Recalling those events today, one year later, I
realize how God has been beside me every step of
the way. Had Christ not been the center of my
life, preparing me and comforting me throughout
this tragedy, I question whether I would be here
to share this story. Although I feel sorrow for
Tom and his family, I have found peace.

As I look back on my life with Tom, I now see
how we both had struggled in unrest with God. I
am thankful that I found that rest when I accepted
Jesus as my much-needed Savior. Sending Tom
the invitation to the crusade was the only way to
show him that he was loved with the ultimate

love—Jesus' love. I will forever hope that Tom accepted Christ as his Savior before he died, but I may never know, for Tom's salvation is between the Lord and him.

What I do know is that God has shown me more grace, forgiveness and unconditional love than I ever deserved, and for this I am—and shall be—eternally grateful.

KATIE PHELPS grew up the oldest of five children in a southern California suburb with dreams of the perfect husband and family. A short but life-changing marriage led to trauma, pain and finally spiritual growth. Katie now speaks to women of all ages on the realistic plans God has for marriage and the sacred nature of wedding vows. At the time Katie wrote this account, she was in the process of relocating from California to Nashville, Tennessee, to pursue a marketing career with a leader in the gift industry.

CHAPTER 11

BOUNCE BACK FROM HARBORED RESENTMENT

*H*ow easy it is to fall into the habit of nursing resentment. We feel perfectly justified because *we* have been "wronged." When we can't find forgiveness in our own hearts, we can turn the matter over to God and ask Him to do the forgiving. The stories in this chapter tell of how each of these writers struggled with lingering resentment and how they were finally able to overcome it by listening to God as He spoke to them in Scripture and through the Holy Spirit.

Therefore, rid yourselves of all malice and all deceit, hypocrisy, envy, and slander of every kind. Like newborn babies, crave pure spiritual milk, so that by it you may grow up in your salvation. (1 Peter 2:1-2)

A Cup of Forgiveness

Emilie Barnes

*I*t was an unbelievably beautiful spring morning. A golden sun was climbing in a brilliant blue, cloudless sky and the sunlight sparkled in the cool air. Bob and I had decided to have our breakfast out on the patio where our little fountain was dancing amid containers of pansies and mums.

Bob read a page from a devotional for husbands and wives. We chatted about the grandchildren and the garden. Then he pulled out our jar of Mom's Canned Questions. It's a decorated jar full of slips of paper, each containing a question designed to stimulate thought and discussion. We use it often when we have company and when we are by ourselves, and the questions have brought us both tears and laughter as they help us know each other better.

Bob passed the jar to me. I reached in and pulled out a slip. As I read it seemed like dark clouds were rolling in to block the sunshine. My impulse was to say, "Forget it!" and stuff it back in the jar.

What was on the paper?

Just this: "What would you do if you could spend one day with your dad?"

Such a simple question. But the memories it evoked filled my cup with pain, anger and resentment.

You see, my dad was a brilliant man, a creative Viennese chef. He got standing ovations for the food he prepared. I'm told he doted on me as a child and I've inherited some of his creativity in the kitchen.

Yet my dad was also a raging alcoholic. Living in our home meant never knowing when he might explode. One wrong word and the spaghetti sauce was dumped down the toilet. The pots would be whipped off the stove and the plates off the table. There would be shouting and arguments. And although my father never physically abused me, he did take his rage out on my mother and brother.

In response to my father's rage, I almost gave up talking. If saying the wrong thing could trigger an explosion, I reasoned it was better not to say anything at all. I became introverted and fearful, and many times I wished my father dead. When I was eleven, he did die, leaving guilt and resentment hanging over my life long after I thought I'd forgotten.

After my dad died, I still didn't talk much. Bob used to say to me, "Emilie, you've got to talk."

And then wonderful things began to happen in my life. The most important was that Bob introduced me to Jesus and I became a Christian. Then Bob asked me to marry him, and my Jewish mama (who was very wise) surprised me by giving her consent.

After Bob and I were married and I felt secure for the first time in my life, I began to talk. Now I even talk for a living—and there are probably times when Bob wishes I would stop talking!

Our lives went on. Our two children were born and I threw my energies into making a home for us all. The kids grew up and left home. Through an amazing series of events, *More Hours in My Day* became a book, then an exciting ministry.

I didn't think much about my dad. He was in my past, which I had put behind me. I was a Christian, and I knew I was supposed to forgive others. So yes, I forgave my dad—or so I thought.

One day I went to a seminar that Lana Bateman was conducting. I didn't really know what it was about, only that my friend Florence Littauer thought it would be good for anyone. I walked into that room . . . and almost immediately my tears began to flow.

I realized that weekend that I still had a lot of pain concerning my father. I thought I had forgiven him, when in fact I had only boxed up my anger and resentment and stored it away. In order to forgive, I had to bring out that anger and resentment and hand them over to God, trusting Him to take them away from me.

That weekend I began the process of truly forgiving my father. I admitted I needed healing. Even though my dad was dead, I wrote him a letter, pouring out my love and fury, confessing the anger and bitterness I had held so long without knowing it was there.

This was hard work, demanding courage and energy. I poured out my cup of resentment. I let the Lord wash it clean and then knew the wonder of having my cup filled with sparkling forgiveness—for my father and for myself. What a wonderful feeling!

But that was not the end of the story. Shortly after that weekend, someone mentioned my father. I was shocked to feel a quick flash of anger. The resentment was still there, or it had come back.

What was going on? Was that difficult weekend in vain? Hadn't I emptied my cup of bitterness and let God fill it with forgiveness?

Oh yes! The forgiveness I experienced that weekend was real. But now I was learning something very important about my cup of forgiveness. It leaked!

For most of us, forgiveness is an ongoing process, not a "done deal." My cup of forgiveness can be brimming over one day and empty the next—or refilled with bitter resentment over the same hurt I thought I had forgiven.

Forgiveness has a forward motion, more like a couple gracefully waltzing across the room than a dog chasing its tail. I know I can move closer and closer to forgiveness because of what happened with my attitude toward my dad.

Despite the cloud that darkened the breakfast sunshine that morning with Bob, I was learning to fill my cup with forgiveness. When I read that difficult question from the jar, I felt pain, but I had an answer.

What would I do if I could spend a day with my dad?

First of all, I would take his hand, and we would walk and reminisce about when I was a little girl.

I'd tell him, "Oh Daddy, I'm sorry for the terrible things that happened to you and made you the way you were. I know why you drank and were so full of fury. You had pain in your heart from being abandoned when your parents died and from being a Jew in Nazi-occupied Austria and fighting in the war and being shot three times."

If I could spend a day with my dad, I wouldn't deny the pain he caused me. I've finally learned that denying pain hinders forgiveness. I would tell my dad that I love him and thank him for the love he poured on me when he wasn't drinking.

And more than anything else, I would tell my dad that our heavenly Father can cover the hurt and pain and take it from us. I would want him to know my dearest friend, the Lord Jesus Christ, who said, "Forgive, and you will be forgiven" (Luke 6:37).

I have finally come to a place where memories

of my father are no longer a source of bitterness for me. Forgiveness has cleansed the area of my heart where those memories reside. And because that is true, I am confident that other areas can be cleansed as well. Because I know forgiveness works, I am more ready to waltz another round.

 EMILIE BARNES has written twenty-two books and co-authored six cookbooks. She and her husband Bob work full time in their ministry, *More Hours in My Day*, which is also the title of one of Emilie's most popular books. She is an associate editor for *Virtue* magazine. As a practical and inspirational speaker, Emilie travels throughout the United States and Canada. She has shared her creative ideas on such national television and radio programs as *The 700 Club, Trinity Broadcasting Network, The Pat Boone Show, Moody Network, Dr. James Dobson Show, The Home Show* and on many local stations.

Resentment Is in a Class by Itself

Marie Asner

I was always overweight. My parents used food, especially sweets, as a reward for "being good" at home or in school. At age ten, I weighed 110 pounds, the same as a mature woman. It was at this time that students in my grade got a male teacher. He was blonde, blue-eyed and handsome. All the girls had a crush on him, including me, but I was the one subjected to teasing because of the crush.

At that time there was a popular radio program called "Luigi." It was about an Italian immigrant who worked for a man with an overweight daughter named "Rosa." "Rosa" became my nickname for years afterward, and I hated it. Even the handsome teacher began calling me "Rosa," much to the amusement of my classmates. School suddenly became a hated place and my grades began to falter.

I avoided everyone from my school and stayed at home even during the summer months. I ventured out only when I was sure everyone else was at the local swimming pool or at a movie. I was always alone.

My mother either made my dresses or went out and bought them in the large women's section of the local department store. While other girls my age were wearing pretty pastel colors, I wore dark brown, navy blue or black, as these were the colors available in my size.

I couldn't fit into the largest women's gym outfit, so the school gave me special permission to wear a blouse and shorts. No one would choose me for any team. I would be left standing by myself and would help the teacher with attendance. This earned me the added annoyance of being called "teacher's pet." At least when it was time to be weighed by the school nurse, it was done in private.

Probably the worst thing that happened to me at this time was when I joined an adult women's weight loss group at a local church. The leader of this group was one of the Sunday school teachers. If you didn't lose what she thought you should lose during the week, she proclaimed, "God will punish you for overeating." This put such fear in me I starved myself for days, only to overeat just before the meeting. After I shed many tears, my mother finally let me drop out of the group—and bought me a hot fudge sundae on the way home to make me feel better.

As time passed, my weight ballooned. My parents moved during my junior year in high school. They were worried about my making new friends, but I couldn't get away from the old school fast enough. The new school was three times as large. No one knew me and so I wasn't teased. There were other students as fat or fatter than me, and we had an unofficial club.

I gained confidence and lost weight in college. I looked like everyone else, but never forgot those tormented years of childhood. When anyone reminisced about the "fun years in school," I changed the subject. The thought of those years gave me heartburn in more ways than one.

As the years passed, I continued to harbor resentment against my former classmates and wished them dire circumstances. One day I was surprised to receive an invitation to the twenty-fifth reunion of my hated high school class. I couldn't believe anyone would be asking *me* to come back and join the class. I didn't know anyone had my address, but obviously someone had found me. I wavered for months between going and not going. Finally, curiosity won out, and I sent in my acceptance at the last moment.

When I walked into the school gym that evening, no one recognized me. I overheard people talking about whether Marie was going to attend, but I didn't hear the name "Rosa" mentioned once. Two men thought I was another classmate, though I recognized them. Finally I went to the information table and retrieved my name tag—to the amazement of most of the group.

I believe now that it was God who gave me the curiosity and the courage to attend the reunion. That evening I felt at peace with Him and felt the resentment I had harbored for years fading away. These were real people, not demons, and I discovered that many of them had fared badly; many had their own stories of hurts and tragedy—parental abuse, abandonment, unwanted pregnancies, teen marriages, low-paying jobs.

There were many apologies that evening from people who had thought of me through the years and wondered what had happened to me. Had the transfer to the new school been successful? Had I been teased there too? They hoped not and were pleased I decided to return to the old "alma mater" even though I hadn't graduated with them.

Since that twenty-fifth reunion I have kept in touch with several classmates. One thing I have noticed in our correspondence: They are determined that no harmful teasing be done in their families.

Years ago, God gave me a Bible passage to hold in my heart, and it has held true and will hold true: "Surely I am with you always" (Matthew 28:20). Even through a weighty childhood and years of resentment, He didn't leave me, but showed me I could leave resentment behind. And I did.

MARIE ASNER is a church musician, poet and writer living in the Kansas City area. She has had over fifty articles published, plus numerous television and radio appearances and poetry readings. Marie was nominated for a 1995 Kansas Governor's Art Award and the 1995 Mary Roberts Rinehart Award in Poetry. A book titled *The Tree of Life* by Marie Asner and Rochelle Holt will be published in 1997.

Let All Bitterness
Be Taken Away

Stanley C. Baldwin

I loved the people of my church and I
was sure they loved me. Didn't they?
But then why were they so indiffer-
ent to my needs? I couldn't understand it.

I had organized this community church in Ore-
gon about five years before and had been its only
pastor ever since. From the beginning, we had
been a close-knit fellowship and God had blessed
us. Our numbers had doubled and tripled. We had
built our own building debt-free and had already
added on once.

At first I had been what's now called a bi-voca-
tional pastor. I worked a regular job and served
the church on a part-time basis. After a year or so,
I went full time with the church. We agreed that if
the congregation would step out in faith to under-
take my support, I would step out in faith to quit

my job and live on considerably less money than I had been making.

All that was fine, but now we were further on down the road. The church was prospering, but I was still scrimping by on my same inadequate salary. I kept expecting that the next monthly business meeting would bring a change, but an increase was never even discussed. *Ok*, I said to myself, *the annual meeting is coming soon. That's a natural time to review my salary. I'll undoubtedly get a raise.*

The annual meeting came, but my raise didn't.

What's the matter with them? I stormed inwardly. *Can't they see I need more money? Don't they know what it costs to raise a family these days?* My wife Marge and I had four children, and she had plenty to do caring for them without trying to take a job outside the home.

As the situation continued with no end in sight, I became more and more resentful. *I'd like to see them try to get by on my salary*, I thought bitterly.

I could have asked for a raise, of course, and with hindsight, that's probably what I should have done. At the time though, I was not willing to do that. I was not in the ministry for the money. I was serving Christ, and I'd continue to serve Christ if they never paid me a dime.

I shouldn't have to ask them, I said to myself, but that conviction only increased my resentment. I became keenly aware that my once healthy relationship with these people was being poisoned more every day.

"What can I do?" I cried to the Lord again and again. "How long can this continue?"

One day I read in the Scripture, "Get rid of all bitterness, rage and anger, brawling and slander, along with every form of malice. Be kind and compassionate to one another, forgiving each other, just as in Christ God forgave you" (Ephesians 4:31-32).

"There are just two problems with that," I argued. "First, I'm not so sure I can 'get rid' of my bitterness. This has gone on too long and the hurt is too deep. Second, it's still going on, and my forgiving them will do nothing to solve the problem. I need more money!"

I dug out the old King James version. Maybe it would not be so uncompromising in its demand to get rid of my bitterness. "Let all bitterness . . . be put away from you," I read. *Hmmm. "Let it be put away." That sounds like I just have to permit it, not actually do it.*

I decided to check the literal. "Let all bitterness . . . be taken away from you," I read, almost not believing my eyes. The Lord was destroying my first argument. I didn't have to get rid of bitterness on my own. I only had to let go of it, give Him permission to take it away.

The Word of God proved therapeutic that day. As I said yes to God on the issue, it was as though a petcock opened in my soul and the acid of bitterness that was eating me drained out.

My second problem—that forgiving would do nothing to solve my money shortage—remained.

But somehow even that seemed different. Now that I no longer resented the people, I could pray better. Maybe—just maybe—God didn't want me to get a raise. Maybe He had something else in mind and needed this financial dilemma to get my attention. Maybe it was time to move on. How would the Lord ever get me to move away from these people I loved without something like this?

God had been blessing special meetings I presented in other churches. Maybe I should become an evangelist. Recently I had published my first article in *Eternity* magazine, circulated nationwide. They had accepted an adaptation of one of my messages. Perhaps God intended me to be a writer.

It was a sad farewell several months later when we left that church. We agreed that we would step out on faith into the unknown if they would step out on faith to find a new pastor. "We don't want you to go, but we are releasing you to a broader ministry," they said as they presented us with a quilt filled with the names of church families.

I was an evangelist only briefly. I later pastored three other churches. I kept writing too and eventually published hundreds of articles and some twenty books. This year I'll teach a dozen writer training seminars in as many states and minister in two foreign countries. I've reaped many blessings I'd never have known if bitterness and resentment had continued to hold me captive.

That church/salary incident was not the last occasion when I thought I had good reason to be resentful. Each time, even though it wasn't easy, I found God was always true to His Word. I didn't have to get rid of my bitterness. I only had to allow Him take it away.

 STANLEY C. BALDWIN is an author and speaker based in Oregon and known internationally. A former editor at Scripture Press and Victor Books, he has written twenty books, including four that have sold some 250,000 copies each. Stan now serves as international editor of *The Christian Communicator*. He has taught writing seminars in Africa, India and Asia as well as across the United States. His books have been translated into eleven languages.

No Room

Marlene Bagnull

I choked back my tears, shrugged my shoulders, pretending indifference and said, "It doesn't matter. We really don't have time to come to the Sunday school class Christmas party anyway." Inside I felt like I had been kicked in the stomach. I had been told that there was "no room" for us.

We'd been members of the church for two years, but I was still struggling with the feeling I didn't belong. It wasn't that people were cold or unfriendly; they just naturally gravitated to their old friends. The fact that I was shy and ill at ease with small talk didn't help.

Through blurred eyes I saw people staring at me. My cheeks flushed with embarrassment as I turned and walked quickly toward the ladies room. Then the tears I could no longer hold back came pouring out. I tried to muffle my sobs in the thickness of my winter coat.

I fumed at myself for waiting until the last minute to sign up. And I knew it was true that the
parsonage could hold only so many people for a
sit-down dinner. But the thought of being turned
away by the church was more than I could handle.
It was the final straw in the battle I'd been fighting for several weeks against "holiday season depression."

My nerves were worn ragged by time pressures
and financial worries. My children were wound
up and uncooperative. I even heard myself echo-
ing the threats I'd heard myself as a child, "If
you're not good, Santa won't come." How clearly
I remembered the Christmas Eve I cried myself to
sleep, knowing I hadn't been good enough, and
convinced there would be nothing under the tree
for me the next morning.

Other painful memories which I usually managed to keep deeply buried burst through the
surface—the loneliness of that first Christmas
after my father died, the school parties I wasn't
invited to attend, the estrangement between my
mother and me. Two years had passed since I
had seen her and, despite my invitation that she
come to spend Christmas with us, I fully expected to be rebuffed again. There was no room
in my mother's life for me and no room in this
church for me.

"Daddy's waiting, Mommie," called my little
daughter. Quickly I dabbed at my eyes. I didn't
want to spoil the day for my family. We planned
to have lunch in a restaurant and then go together

to choose and cut down our Christmas tree. Both eleven-year-old Debbie and six-year-old Robbie had been counting the days till this event. Even Sharon, our ever-busy teenager, had made a place in her schedule to spend the afternoon with us.

I glanced in the mirror at my puffy eyes. I bit my trembling lip and struggled to keep my feelings out of sight.

My family's happy chatter could not break my bleakness as we climbed into the car. My husband squeezed my hand.

"What's the matter, hon?" he said.

"Nothing," I mumbled, turning my head so he couldn't see the tear sliding down my cheek.

We tramped through the woods together in search of the perfect tree. To his delight, Robbie was the one who found it; a tall, fat, bushy white pine—just what we wanted. Pride shone in his eyes as he helped his father drag it to the car.

The next day I sank deeper into my pit of self-pity and despair. I moved like a robot in slow motion making the beds and doing the laundry. I couldn't bring myself to write Christmas cards or bake cookies.

Suddenly I clearly felt the Lord speaking to me in that quiet inner voice.

"There was no room for Me either," He seemed to say.

I was stunned by the thought. A familiar Scripture entered my mind: "Although he made the world, the world didn't recognize him when he came. Even in his own land and among his own people, the Jews, he was not accepted. Only a few would welcome and receive him" (John 1:10-12, TLB).

With new awareness, I recalled the innkeeper declaring "no room" on the night of Jesus' birth, and I thought how those words were just the beginning of the rejection and pain that lay ahead for Him. I thought of how the religious leaders harrassed Him, His own brothers ridiculed Him and many of His disciples turned away and deserted Him.

"Oh Jesus, how did You handle the hurt and pain?" I asked. I closed my eyes and sighed.

Suddenly I envisioned the Lord sitting alone beside a rushing stream. His shoulders were hunched and His face was in His hands. Slowly He raised His head. I saw the tiredness in His eyes and the stain of a tear down His cheek. I felt the hurt and pain He had endured. But then I felt His love and compassion as He looked at me and smiled.

The answer to my question flashed into my mind—clear and unmistakable: Just as Jesus went to the Father and received strength, I am to go to Him. He said, "Come to me, all you who are weary and burdened. I know how you feel because I've been there first" (see Matthew 11:28).

As my thoughts returned momentarily to the situation at church and the relationship with my mother, He gently reminded me, "You don't have to worry about anything, because you can pray about everything" (see Philippians 4:6-7). I put those worries into the Lord's outstretched hands and felt the peace He promised. It was more wonderful than I could understand.

In that instant I recaptured the joy and understood the real meaning of Christmas: God so loved the world that He gave His only Son. The Son came and lived among us, *choosing to love and forgive those who rejected Him.*

"Oh, come to my heart, Lord Jesus," I prayed. "There is room in my heart for Thee."*

That prayer became a turning point. I stopped feeling sorry for myself, and in the days that followed began to prepare enthusiastically for Christmas. When I changed, everything else seemed to change too.

A letter came from my mother saying she was coming to spend Christmas with us!

The pastor of our church called. "I'm so sorry about what happened," he said. "We don't ever want to turn anyone away. We're moving the dinner to the church fellowship hall so there will be room for everyone."

This time tears of joy spilled down my cheeks—not just because there was room for me in my church and in my mother's life, but most importantly because of the way God had used this experience to give me a new awareness of what His Son endured when there was no room for Him.

* Emily E.S. Elliot (1836-1897), from the hymn "Thou Didst Leave Thy Throne."

MARLENE BAGNULL believes that problems are grist for her "writer's mill" and an opportunity to share with others the difference Jesus Christ makes. She has written for numerous Christian periodicals, authored four books and compiled *My Turn to Care—Affirmations for Caregivers of Aging Parents*. Marlene lives in Drexel Hill, Pennsylvania and is a frequent speaker at Christian writers' conferences around the nation.

CHAPTER 12

HELP OTHERS BOUNCE BACK

*T*he encouragement and support we give to others in times of trouble can make the difference between hope and hopelessness. With the compassion of Jesus as our example, we can be a beneficial presence to all whose paths we cross. Sometimes we can help in tangible ways. We can also help in intangible ways by showing compassion and caring and by lifting that distressed or needy friend to God in fervent prayer. The stories related in this chapter give touching and inspiring proof that, with God's help, we can help others move forward or bounce back.

Whatever you did for one of the least of these brothers of mine, you did for me. (Matthew 25:40)

With a Little Help from My Friends

Elizabeth Jeffries

It's not that I grew up in a home without God. It's just that the God I knew was a God of judgment! I was very scared of this God-Person. My friends had some rules that I didn't understand. I just knew if I didn't obey them I would go to hell.

I learned my faith by memorizing the answers to the questions in the Baltimore Catechism. A good way to start, except the answers stayed in my head—and when they did get to my heart, it was with shame, blame and guilt. It seems I was always told about what would happen if I didn't obey. So I became, externally, a very obedient child. I went to church, confessed my sins on Saturday, gave up candy for Lent and performed all the rituals expected of me. God always seemed to be a God of "no" and rarely a God of "yes." Figuring I could never measure up to what was expected of me, I ended up avoiding God altogether.

I married a good man but, with no spiritual bond between us, we drifted apart. Even though we had a life of external success, I was dying inside. Wandering in a spiritual desert, I drifted into friendships with people who, like me, were unhappy in their marriages. Mother was right, "You are the company you keep." My lifestyle was such that I could have been the Samaritan woman at Jacob's well. Sometimes though, you have to break down before you break through. Determined to change, I began the next phase of my life as a seeker.

A friend convinced me to attend church. I attended, all right, but I didn't attend to the Christian life. I participated in the services, but I still didn't listen to the Spirit working in my heart.

I also explored other avenues of spirituality. I went to an Ashram regularly and became fascinated with Eastern tradition. I immersed myself in New Age thinking and practices. While it wasn't Christianity, it did help me to think about God again—or my "higher power" as I safely called it.

In the midst of all this, I started a speaking and consulting business and joined the National Speakers Association. In 1988, Naomi Rhode, one of our esteemed members, spoke at an NSA meeting. She told us about the time when, after undergoing a breast biopsy, she woke up to find it was benign and that her friends had put a banner over her bed proclaiming "To God Be the Glory." I was blown away that she would say the "G word" right there on the platform!

Later at that meeting, I asked Naomi, "How are you able to talk about God so freely from the platform?" That question changed my life! Naomi became my spiritual godmother. She encouraged me, modeled Christian love and talked about Jesus.

Now wait a minute! It's one thing to say "God." It's another to speak the name of Jesus. I could hardly get that name out of my mouth! It stuck in my throat like a peanut butter and jelly sandwich before it's washed down with milk.

From that beginning with Naomi, the Christian friends I have made opened the door to the Light. We've held hands and prayed for each other in our moment of need, sent notes of encouragement to each other by mail, exchanged information for Bible study by fax and even prayed together by phone and e-mail.

Friends came across the country in 1992 to celebrate my marriage to my best friend, Stephen Tweed, the most loving and godly man I know. They came again in 1995 as together we were immersed in the waters of baptism.

My sister in Christ, Liz Curtis Higgs, is a woman with a dramatic conversion. In spite of her busy speaking schedule, it was Liz who suggested Stephen and I join her and Bill for a Bible study on Sunday nights. Miraculously, God coordinated our schedules to fit.

I've never had a dramatic conversion like Paul on the road to Damascus. No thunderbolt. No one moment when I can say I accepted Jesus as my personal Savior. Rather there have been a series of them. I've always known *about* Jesus. Now I'm getting to *know* Jesus, my personal Lord and Savior. I know that by His grace, I am His child. I now understand the words to the hymn which say, "I walk with Him and I talk with Him . . ." because He is with me all day. When I'm stuck, I ask myself, *What would Jesus do?* and the answer is always there.

I'm just beginning to understand what it means to be a follower of Christ. To me it means surrender, and I admit I have a tough time with that. I'm a strong-willed woman. As I ask Christ to change me and as I learn to surrender, He is blessing me in ways I don't always understand at the moment. Sometimes I think I'm on a path that is His will and then He points me in another direction.

Like the National Speakers Association. I joined in 1983. I was in a leadership role for thirteen years, with six of those on the national board holding the office of secretary, then treasurer. Next step was vice-president, which would automatically put me in line to become president of NSA.

Then God said no. So I obeyed and declined the nomination, even though my ego really wanted to be president of this prestigious organization of 3,500 members.

Now what, God? I promised to follow You whereever

You lead me. So I will trust You and live in the excitement that You will use me in a way that will glorify You and not me, in a way that will feed Your flock and not my ego.

See, God, I remember in 1990 when I was trying to straighten out my personal life as a single woman. I started into a relationship that was not pleasing to You. You gave me the strength to turn away from it, and in the next breath You gave me the most precious Christian man who was to be my husband and walk with me on our spiritual path forever. Now we worship You together. You need not prove anything to me ever again!

I have a favorite African violet in my kitchen that suddenly just stopped blooming. I tried everything to revive it. I became so frustrated that I almost threw it away. Looking around the kitchen one sunny morning, I noticed a spot where the light was shining in. I moved the plant there and waited.

A month passed and nothing happened. *Ok, I'll wait a bit longer. . . .* Then one morning, while I was watering the violet, I noticed clusters of tiny buds! I knelt on the floor in the stream of bright sunlight as it poured through the window.

Not only was I grateful for the new flower buds, but I felt so grateful that God is patient with me, that He didn't throw me away because I wasn't blooming, that He waited while my friends watered me, nurtured me and prayed for me. Theirs were the loving, encouraging hands that picked me up and moved me from a dark windowsill into the Light.

ELIZABETH JEFFRIES, CPS (Certified Professional Speaker,) is a professional speaker, seminar leader, consultant and author on leadership and change strategies. She is based in Louisville, Kentucky. Specializing in servant leadership, she guides individuals and teams to *live and lead from the inside out*. Elizabeth has experienced many changes since renewing her Christian faith. She moved from not understanding what an "altar call" was to answering one in January 1995, and from being immersed in her business to being immersed in the baptismal waters in March, 1995. She had always prided herself on being a woman in control, but now she celebrates being a woman under God's control.

Freddy

Robin Ashford

*I*t was another first day at school. I introduced myself, had the students introduce themselves, passed out the books and syllabi, then gave the first lecture.

They were each starting something new with hopes and dreams that at the end they would get a job. It was my job to break them in to the new routines of disciplined study in addition to teaching the first module of material.

A couple of days passed.

Grabbing lunch in the cafeteria, I had just sat down when Freddy stepped up to the table. He was heavyset with curly blond hair, red face, bright blue eyes and big, big grins. Like a big teddy bear.

"Hi!" he bubbled. Grinning. Cheerful. Excited. "I just wanted to let you know that I recently got out of jail and I'm not used to all this studying, but I'm going to work really hard."

We talked some more. He shared. He spoke of
his wife and two daughters. He and his wife had
been in jail. Both had accepted the Lord while in
jail. He got out first and got the kids back. His
wife was due out in another few weeks. He had
found a really good church and was all excited for
God. No job. No care. Might be late occasionally
for class, but he'd be there.

The weeks passed. Freddy worked hard and
kept me posted about his activities at church and
his family.

"My wife is getting out of jail today!!"

More weeks passed. Freddy was no longer my
student but was in the third or fourth module of
classes. Yet he had continued to swing by almost
daily just to say hi and let me know how things
were going with his new life in Christ, his kids, his
mom . . . and I hadn't seen him lately.

I contacted his current instructor—no Freddy.
He'd missed several classes and his homework
was way behind. Although I had been praying occasionally for Freddy and his family I started including him daily.

A couple of days later as I was lecturing I spotted him going down the hall. I gave the class a pop
quiz (wonderful things) and stepped out of the
classroom.

"Freddy, what's up? I haven't seen you around
lately."

"My wife has started doing drugs again and
wants me to join her. She hasn't wanted to go to
church and is really against my involvement and

activities in it. I was going through a twelve-step program and then, when she got out, she wanted to go too. But, they wouldn't let her start in the middle. So I dropped out to wait for the next one. She gets mean sometimes. . . ."

Listening to Freddy, watching his face, I wondered. I asked him, "Freddy, is she hitting you?"

"Well, she gets angry, and it doesn't hurt much. . . ." He paused. "Anyway, we've only got one car now and I've been letting her use it because she gets bored being stuck at home with the kids. I've been having trouble getting to school in the mornings, but I make it."

More days passed. And again—no Freddy. No Freddy for one day . . . two days . . . three days . . . four days. I felt a strong urge to pray for Freddy and his family. Into the next week and still no Freddy. I thought I might have to go knock on his door, but I was totally swamped at work, so I just prayed—and prayed—and prayed.

Weeks passed—and I prayed.

More weeks passed. I figured I would not be seeing Freddy again, but kept getting a burden to pray for him, his wife, their daughters.

Prayed.

Some months had gone by. I was working at my desk; the students were out working on the computers in the lab. Noise. I looked up. Striding in to the room was—Freddy!

"I'm back!" he said with that big ol' grin on his face. "I dropped out for awhile. My wife got back into doing drugs and wanted me to do them with her. I dropped out of church . . . dropped out of school. But things just didn't work out. I tried to meet her where she was at—and then the next counseling session started and she wouldn't go. She wouldn't go to church either. I was just miserable, so I moved out.

"I'm staying on a couch at my aunt's house. Some brothers at church come by and give me rides to and from church. I'm back into Bible study and going to the sessions.

"Sometimes I've got to walk a lot, but—it's great!

"I try to visit and spend time with my daughters and reassure them. I just love my family, but I'm not going to do the drugs and drop out of church like my wife wants me to. Things are more peaceful now. My wife still gets upset. But I'm *back!* And I'm not leaving God again."

I congratulated Freddy. Then I encouraged him. I said, "Your wife is in a big battle. Your family is in a battle. But you can win, Freddy. Just hang in there. Pray. Take authority in prayer over your family. Stick close to Jesus. And love, love, love them."

Freddy left grinning.

I thanked God for allowing me to see one result of the prayer burden and prayer for a student. I had a strong sense that without prayer Freddy would not have made it back—the prayers of his church, his pastor, his new friends and me.

Welcome back, Freddy!

Now for his family . . .

ROBIN K. ASHFORD (pen name Caitlin O'Shaunessy) is a budding freelance writer, speaker and regular contributing author to The *Christian Communicator.* As an adjunct college professor in San Diego with a passion for seeing students grow, she teaches a variety of office automation, computer and business courses with liberal doses of humor. Robin has provided administrative and computer assistance at several Christian writers conferences over the past six years.

I Didn't Have A Prayer

Diana L. James

One early spring evening several years ago I stood at the window of my apartment and gazed at the cemetery across the driveway. A cool breeze brushed my arm, breaking my reverie.

I looked down at the Bible in my hands. Its white leather cover seemed to glow in the soft light that sifted through the window. This Bible had been my mother's until she died the year before. After her death, I found comfort in its pages and in the memory of my childhood when she had read it to me as I snuggled by her side.

But lately this old friend had become a stranger. I hadn't been able to bring myself to open it or quote a Scripture or even say a prayer. My spiritual numbness had started four months earlier, when my husband Roger was killed in an airplane accident.

Trying to put my thoughts in order, I walked across the darkening room and settled on the sofa. Suddenly, a soft "meow" broke my concentration. My orange-and-white tabby cat Leo rubbed against me as if to say, "Don't feel bad; I'm here."

Leo was one of the few creatures who sensed I was hurting. My four grown sons were out in the world on their own, so I lived alone with Leo. It was only in our solitude that I let my unhappiness show; at work, I smiled confidently.

When Roger died, I had taken over his business: a funeral home in northern California. My new role as funeral director required giving comfort to others during their bereavement. Now I found myself *among* the bereaved, but could not reverse my role as giver of comfort to that of taker of comfort. When friends asked how I was doing, I answered, "Just fine." I was so determined to be strong that I had not shed one tear since Roger's funeral. It was the first time in my life I couldn't cry.

At the same time I was managing the business, I was enveloped in a web of legal and financial problems. It appeared that I would lose the funeral home because of a clerical error in the wording of the deed. It became necessary for me to sell many possessions just to make ends meet.

As I sat there that evening with the Bible on my lap, the doorbell rang. I opened the door and let in my close friend Irene. "How are you doing?" she asked, her worried eyes trying to penetrate the wall I'd built around my emotions.

"There's something wrong," I admitted as I looked down at my Bible. "I haven't been able to cry or even pray since Roger died."

"Would it help if I said the words for you?" Irene asked softly. I was willing to try it. We knelt by the sofa. She was silent for a long time, then said, "Lord, I need Your help." I waited for more words. Irene's simple prayer did not seem adequate. I had expected something more eloquent, like the formal prayers I had prayed myself until these past four months.

Then, slowly, an urgent sense of dependence on the Father began forming inside me. Suddenly, through me burst those words: "Lord, I need Your help!" Almost before I finished this prayer, a sob came from deep inside me and tears began to flow.

Today, when I reflect on that period of my life, I am grateful for friends such as Irene who helped me begin a new prayer life. Irene's brief prayer helped me focus on *what* I wanted to say, instead of *how* to say it. I saw that, even in the numbness of my grief, I could pray simple prayers, and these were more sincere than many I had prayed before.

I searched for and found many biblical stories showing the power of a short, simple prayer. An example was the repentant tax collector who did not pray like the pompous Pharisee, but instead said, "God, have mercy on me, a sinner" (Luke 18:13). And then there was the blind beggar who cried out when he heard Jesus passing by. When Jesus asked what he wanted the beggar replied:

"Lord, I want to see" (Luke 18:41). And Jesus answered his prayer.

When my prayers became shorter, I found I was taking more time to listen for God's answers. God often speaks to me in a very quiet voice, so I learned to concentrate on keeping my mind open to hear Him. I thought of the verse, "Speak, LORD; for thy servant heareth" (1 Samuel 3:9, KJV). In the past, it seemed I had been saying, "Listen, Lord, for Your servant speaketh."

Two-way prayer, speaking and listening, helped me in many ways. One night during my recovery period, I prayed fervently for a fair resolution to all the legal problems. The quiet inner voice said, "The answer is on the way." A few days later, I received an invitation to a Christian conference in southern California. Since I felt this invitation had to be my "answer," I went to the conference.

My legal problems weren't solved immediately, but the conference was indeed a turning point for me. Several months later, I left the funeral home in the hands of my loyal staff, moved to southern California and accepted a challenging, exciting new job in Christian leadership.

There I also met Max James, who later became my husband.

My spiritual life began to grow deeper and richer. Max led me through a compassionate and freeing process of prayer and guided meditation that helped me erase the frightful nightmares I was having about Roger's plane crash. Together, we found opportunities to minister to others' needs, both tangibly and spiritually. Friends had helped me during my spiritual crisis, and now I found joy in doing the same for others. I filled my prayers with other people's needs. I prayed for the bereaved funeral home clients, for the people at my church, my friends and relatives and for world leaders.

Max and I faced a tough decision: whether or not to move back to northern California to try to resolve the problems with my business. We sought God's guidance together and separately about this decision. God's answer came independently to each of us: *Go back.* Obediently we moved back to northern California where Max helped me unravel the legal and financial problems of the funeral home.

I finally received a clear title to the business, and we ministered there, helping families face the trauma of death. After three years we sold the funeral home, then moved back to southern California to wait for further leading from above.

We were led to accept positions as resident managers of a Christian retreat center. As the Lord used us in this ministry, He also opened another area where He wanted me to serve. I was asked to speak on *prayer* for Christian retreats and workshops. After attending CLASS (Christian Leaders, Authors and Speakers Seminars), Inc., I also began speaking professionally on grief and loss for businesses, bereavement groups and funeral associations across the U.S.

My lifelong concern for children has also led me to speak and write on the subject of children's bereavement—a field where there is a great need for knowledge, understanding and compassion.

I am so thankful for the opportunities I have now to serve the Lord by serving others, especially since I can still remember the time when it seemed I didn't have a prayer.

DIANA L. JAMES' articles and stories have appeared in *Parents Magazine, The Christian Communicator, Jack and Jill, Today's Christian Woman* and many other publications, including four anthology books. Diana was host/moderator of a weekly TV interview program for five years. She was also administrator and district supervisor for recreation departments in two large cities in northern California. Currently, Diana lives in Laguna Hills, California. She writes and speaks on recovery from grief and loss. She recently produced an audio tape titled, *What Do We Tell the Children?* which is used by hospice and bereavement groups to help parents and children work through the experience of loss.

Create in me a pure heart, O God, and renew a steadfast spirit within me. Do not cast me from your presence or take your Holy Spirit from me. Restore to me the joy of your salvation and grant me a willing spirit, to sustain me. (Psalm 51:10-12)